CENTURY
BHOYS

PAUL CUDDIHY AND DAVID FRIEL

CENTURY BHOYS

THE OFFICIAL HISTORY OF CELTIC'S GREATEST GOALSCORERS

BLACK & WHITE PUBLISHING

First published 2010
by Black & White Publishing Ltd
29 Ocean Drive, Edinburgh EH6 6JL

1 3 5 7 9 10 8 6 4 2   10 11 12 13

ISBN: 978 1 84502 297 6

A CII

Print

CONTENTS

ACKNOWLEDGEMENTS

I'm always envious of anyone lucky enough even to have worn the Hoops for five minutes, never mind actually score a goal for Celtic, so to be able to write about the twenty-eight players who have scored over 100 goals for the club since 1888 has been a real privilege.

Both David Friel and I would like to thank Black & White Publishing for their faith in this project which, as Celtic supporters, we've thoroughly enjoyed writing. David was the consummate professional in completing the manuscript and I'd like to thank him for all his help. I also think he's finally come to accept that his football knowledge isn't second to none, and that the Inverness quiz result proves this.

My family always show great understanding during these writing projects and, as always, I want to thank Karen and our children, Louise, Rebecca and Andrew.

Paul Cuddihy

I would like to thank my Mum and Dad, Philip and Kathleen, for their love, support and guidance over the last twenty-nine years. I truly couldn't have asked for better parents. Thanks also to Philip, John, Geraldine, Mairi, James, the other members of the ever-expanding Friel family and all the St Maurice's boys.

Thanks go to the entire Celtic multi-media team, office staff, management and players for giving me the best four years of my working life at the Celtic View. Special mention to the inimitable Gregor Kyle – the Little of our Little and Large combo – for his encouragement and friendship. And, of course, thanks to Paul Cuddihy for being the Lennon to my McCartney on this book.

A big thanks to the twenty-eight Century Bhoys, especially the inspirational John Hartson and my distant relation Jimmy Quinn, for scoring so many goals for Celtic and making this book possible.

And last, but by no means least, I'd like to express my love and thanks to my girlfriend Emma for her unique love, support and encouragement.

David Friel

INTRODUCTION

It was Mark Twain who famously said 'lies, damned lies and statistics,' but while the American author was using it to illustrate the way that numbers can be manipulated to back up an otherwise weak argument, when it comes to Celtic goalscoring statistics, they can serve to strengthen the case for a player's quality, his contribution to the club and, indeed, his greatness within the pantheon of Celtic legends.

Since Celtic's first ever competitive game, a Scottish Cup first-round tie against Shettleston on 1 September 1888, a total of 798 players up to May 2010 have represented the club at first-team level.

In the same period, Celtic has scored 11,052 competitive goals. These goals have helped the club win 42 league championships, 34 Scottish Cups, 14 League Cups and one European Cup.

However, in almost 122 years, only 28 players have managed to score more than 100 competitive goals for Celtic.

These men, to throw out a statistic, represent just 3.5% of the number of players to have pulled on, at various times, the all-white top with the Celtic cross, the green and white stripes, the more famous green and white Hoops, along with a whole host of away shirts of varying colours, designs and taste.

It is an illustrious band of footballing brothers and, not surprisingly, they can all be regarded as great Celtic players to one degree or another. Their contribution came in goals, games and bringing success to the football club and it is their exploits which will continue to be recounted in the history books.

Of course, football is a team game and a goalscorer needs a provider, and that's where the other 770 players come in. Again, that's not to downplay their importance to the Celtic story.

For example, has anyone made a greater contribution to the cause than Billy McNeill? He may only have scored 35 goals but they came in an unrivalled 790 competitive appearances for the club, and he was the captain who led Celtic to nine league titles in a row and victory on May 25, 1967, which confirmed the club as the Champions of Europe.

This book, however, is a celebration of the Century Bhoys, the 28 men who hit 100 goals or more for Celtic.

They are led by the peerless Jimmy McGrory. Celtic supporters know their history and they know that there never was, nor ever will be, a better goalscorer than the Bhoy born in the Garngad district of Glasgow. Of all the flowers that sprouted forth in that 'Garden of God', none bloomed as fruitfully nor as brightly as James Edward McGrory.

He scored 468 goals in 445 appearances for Celtic, a total that is 195 ahead of Bobby Lennox, the club's second top goalscorer of all time. Lennox's tally, in itself, is an impressive one and came during the club's golden era of the late 1960s and early 1970s when Celtic dominated Scottish football and were one of the best teams in Europe.

The fact that his teammates Stevie Chalmers, Jimmy Johnstone, Willie Wallace, Bobby Murdoch and John Hughes also hit over 100 goals is an indication of Celtic's attacking potency at that time.

If Jimmy McGrory is the greatest of them all, then Sandy McMahon led the way in becoming the first Celtic player to score over 100 goals for the club. McMahon played for the club between

1890 and 1903, and can rightly stake a claim to be the first Celtic Great as well.

He played in the club's first trophy triumphs – the Scottish Cup win in 1892 and the first league championship a year later – but he left Celtic before the famous six-in-a-row success between 1905 and 1910, and also departed just before the club changed their kit to the famous Hoops.

Sandy McMahon was one of the greatest players ever to play for Celtic and one of the greatest *never* to wear the green and white Hoops.

The twenty-first century has seen two new additions to the Century Bhoys, with Henrik Larsson and John Hartson both reaching impressive milestones. In Hartson's case that was 110 goals, while Larsson, in seven seasons at the club, scored 242 goals to become Celtic's third top goalscorer of all time.

There have been other players, of course, and each one merits a mention in his own right – or a chapter in this case. Jimmy Quinn, Patsy Gallacher, Jimmy McMenemy, Kenny Dalglish, Adam McLean, Tommy McInally, Charlie Nicholas, Dixie Deans, Jimmy McColl, Harry Hood, Brian McClair, Bobby Collins, Johnny Campbell, Neilly Mochan, Frank McGarvey, Joe Cassidy, Alec Thomson and John Divers are the men who make up the remainder of the twenty-eight Century Bhoys.

Every story is unique and each achievement is remarkable on its own, but together they have helped to shape Celtic Football Club and have set the standards that others will strive to achieve ... and possibly surpass. There will be other Century Bhoys in the future but, for now, these twenty-eight men form this exclusive group and their statistics don't lie. They merely confirm their collective status as Celtic Greats.

1

JIMMY McGRORY

468 GOALS IN 445 APPEARANCES

Jimmy McGrory is the greatest goalscorer ever to play for Celtic. That is a statement unlikely to be contradicted as long as the football club exists. He scored 468 goals in 445 games. That's 192 more goals than the second top scorer of all time, Bobby Lennox. Indeed, if you combined Lennox's tally with that of Patsy Gallacher's they would only equal McGrory's.

It would be easy to fill this chapter with statistics to try and give a proper sense of what can only be described as a goalscoring phenomenon, but they can only scratch at the surface of a remarkable player. It's like trying to describe St Peter's Basilica in Rome to someone who hasn't actually been inside it.

Yet, even a cursory glance at the history books can almost take the breath away. Jimmy McGrory scored five goals in a single game on no fewer than four occasions. In eleven different matches, he netted four goals, and he produced an incredible *thirty-nine* hat-tricks during the fifteen years he played for his beloved green and white Hoops.

In *The Story of the Celtic*, Willie Maley said of Jimmy McGrory:

With all respect to the many other splendid Celts we have had and still have, I want to say this: We have never had, unless with one exception, a player whose prowess and o'erflowing enthusiasm have led us to so many victories.

1

The exception is Paddy Gallacher. As a goal-getter McGrory stands supreme. He has scored more goals with his head than any other player. Celtic have had many offers for his transfer. Arsenal wanted him very much. We left it to him to say 'Yes' or 'No'. 'No' it was. He wanted to finish his playing career with Celtic.

Maley was undoubtedly a fan of McGrory's, and would certainly have appreciated his contribution over the many years he was at the club, though it could be argued that he was being economical with the truth when it came to explaining away Arsenal's interest in signing the player.

The general consensus was that it was Celtic who were instrumental in trying to sell McGrory to the London club and that they had arranged 'surprise' encounters at Euston Station, London, with Arsenal manager, Herbert Chapman, when Maley and McGrory were travelling to and from Lourdes.

Maley had also noted of McGrory in his book that, 'his heart was ours long before he was offered a peg in our dressing room,' and thankfully for the Celtic supporters that was indeed the case, with the Garngad Bhoy rejecting all overtures from Arsenal, even to the point of signing a contract with Celtic that saw him paid one pound less than other players.

In twelve of the thirteen seasons he played in, when he returned to the club in 1924 after a successful loan spell with Clydebank, he was the club's top goalscorer, breaking all previous scoring records and setting new ones that would never be beaten.

Twice he was also Europe's leading goalscorer, in 1926/27 (49 goals) and 1935/36 (50 goals). And, as well as all the singles, doubles, trebles, quadruples and quintuples on 14 January 1928, he scored *eight* goals in a 9–0 victory over Dunfermline Athletic. Willie Maley was certainly right about one thing: 'As a goal-getter, McGrory stands supreme.'

FIRST GOAL

It was on 3 February 1923 that Jimmy McGrory first hit the back of the net for Celtic. The teenage striker, just two months short of his nineteenth birthday, scored after ten minutes for the defending champions, but it was a game that Celtic would lose 4–3, while they would also relinquish their league title that season, finishing third in the table.

The young McGrory made a total of four appearances that first season – three in the league and one in the Scottish Cup against Lochgelly United – and his goal against Kilmarnock was his only one of the campaign

He had signed for Celtic in June 1921 and made his debut just less than two years later, in a 1–0 defeat away to Third Lanark.

Season 1923/24 saw him loaned out to Clydebank where, under the leadership of former Celt, Jimmy 'Dun' Hay, he began to blossom as a centre forward, scoring twenty-three goals for the Bankies that season, including one against the Hoops at Celtic Park on 4 March 1924, when Clydebank won 2–1. It was, McGrory later said, 'the goal that reminded Celtic I existed.'

He established himself in the Celtic first team from the start of season 1924/25, taking over as the main goal threat from another Century Bhoy, Joe Cassidy, who had left the club in 1923, having netted 103 goals.

McGrory later acknowledged Cassidy's role in teaching him the art of heading a ball, and the pupil quickly became the master as there can have been few finer exponents of heading a ball than Jimmy McGrory.

While he had succeeded Cassidy in becoming the main provider of goals for the team, he was viewed as the natural successor to Jimmy Quinn in terms of being a combative and prolific centre forward.

Having chalked up his first goal for Celtic, and then proving his ability at Clydebank, McGrory now set about his goalscoring task in the Hoops with relish. In that first season back at Celtic Park, he scored twenty-eight goals and followed it up with forty-two the following season.

Unsurprisingly, Celtic won the title that season for the first time since 1922, though they relinquished the Scottish Cup they'd won the year before, losing to St Mirren in the final. But the honours would not flow to Celtic Park as might have been expected, given the goal machine now playing in the green and white Hoops.

100TH GOAL

It took Jimmy McGrory almost four years to score his 100th goal, though that included a season when he only made four appearances for the club and a season on loan at Clydebank. The goal that made him a Century Bhoy came on 8 January 1927, in a game against Morton at Cappielow. He scored ten minutes from time to put Celtic 5–2 up in a match that the home side had actually taken the lead in after just twelve minutes.

McGrory had already scored one goal in that game, after seventy minutes, while fellow Century Bhoy, Tommy McInally, also weighed in with two goals that day against a side that would finish second-bottom of the table at the end of the season. Celtic would finish a disappointing third, despite McGrory hitting forty-nine league goals in the campaign to become Europe's top goalscorer that season.

He scored just under half of Celtic's league goals in the campaign – the Hoops netted an impressive 101 goals – but the team lost too many games, including both league meetings with Rangers, and were seven points behind the Ibrox side.

Once again, it was the Scottish Cup which provided a modicum of consolation for the Celtic supporters, with East Fife defeated 3–1 in the final.

Celtic were blessed with some exceptional players in the early 1920s, with McGrory joining a club that could call upon the talents of Patsy Gallacher and Tommy McInally, to name but two. However, Gallacher was allowed to leave the club in 1926 for Falkirk, while McInally's personality and tumultuous relationship with Willie Maley eventually saw him exit two years later, having failed to truly utilise the footballing talents he so evidently possessed.

McGrory remained 'faithful through and through', a concept alien in today's game, particularly when one considers that he was effectively 'punished' for not joining Arsenal by being given a lower wage for the remainder of his Celtic career.

That the club would do that to one of its greatest players and most faithful servants seems hard to imagine, but such was the nature of Celtic, and indeed, football at the time.

It didn't stop the player scoring, however, and the eight goals he did score in 1928 remain a British record for the number of goals scored by an individual player in a top-flight match.

Celtic striker Dixie Deans came close to equalling it in November 1973 when he scored six goals in a match against Partick Thistle.

After the game, as the players made their way towards the dressing room, Jimmy McGrory was inside waiting for Deans, telling the striker: 'Son, I really thought you were going to take my record there!'

LAST GOAL

On 16 October 1937, Celtic beat Queen's Park 4–3 and a crowd of 12,000 witnessed Jimmy McGrory's last goal for his beloved

Hoops. There wouldn't have been many, if any at all, who would have seen the previous 467, while no one who cheered that goal would have realised it would be the last time they would see something that had become as natural to their lives as day and night.

McGrory scored five goals that season, his last for the club, as Celtic regained the league title, finishing three points clear of second-placed Hearts.

It was a season for supporters to celebrate, though it was one in which another player, in this case Johnny Crum, finished as the club's top goalscorer, netting twenty-five.

The season was also the last hurrah for Celtic's legendary manager Willie Maley. Maley had been a part of Celtic Football Club since he had played in the club's very first game – a 5–2 victory over Rangers on 28 May 1888 – and he had managed the team since 1897.

As the twenty-first century beckoned, Celtic supporters would sing a song in his honour, acknowledging the contribution he had made to the club that has only been rivalled by Jock Stein.

The 'Willie Maley Song' celebrates the fact the former manager 'brought some great names to the game', and there were plenty in those first fifty years of the club's existence.

There were few, if any, who were greater than Jimmy McGrory, and it's his name which takes pride of place as the first to be mentioned in the chorus. For, having scored 468 goals in 445 games, outgunning anyone who had gone before or who has come since to play for the club, McGrory fully deserves his place in the folklore of the club and he can stand proudly in the pantheon of Celtic Greats.

If there is one regret, it's that his goalscoring feats were never captured on camera because what a sight that must have been to behold.

And it's also appropriate that Jimmy McGrory's last goal

should also have come in his final game for Celtic. He was a man who gave everything to the green and white Hoops he loved and he bowed out as a player in a manner befitting the club's greatest ever goalscorer ... with a final goal for Celtic.

HIGHS AND LOWS

There are so many individual Jimmy McGrory performances to highlight that it would be difficult to focus on any in particular, though his eight goals in one game remain an incredible and unmatched feat.

He didn't win as many honours for Celtic as he should have. There were only three league championships, in 1926, 1936 and 1938, while there were also five Scottish Cups – 1925, 1927, 1931, 1933 and 1937 – and it was in the first of these finals that the young striker began to make his mark.

The 1925 Scottish Cup final will forever be known as 'The Patsy Gallacher Final' for the Irishman's acrobatics to score Celtic's equaliser. But it was McGrory's header with three minutes of the match remaining which won the cup for the Hoops.

Like every player of that generation, whatever highs that might have been achieved were overshadowed by the most terrible of lows, and Jimmy McGrory, along with his Celtic teammates, was devastated by the tragic death of goalkeeper John Thomson on 5 September 1931.

Speaking in 2007 during a visit to Celtic Park, McGrory's daughter, Maria Graham, spoke about her father. She said:

To everybody else he was a Celtic legend but he never played that side up and, to us, he was always just Dad. The biggest story I remember him talking about was Johnny Thomson as he was quite a close friend of his and that had a big effect on him.

Celtic's ultimate goalscorer was an admirer of Celtic's greatest goalkeeper, though the loss he would have felt was as a friend.

Jimmy McGrory would go on to manage Celtic from 1945–65, during which time the club won the league title once in 1953/54, and the Scottish Cup on two occasions, in 1951 and 1954, winning the League Cup in two consecutive seasons, 1956/57 and 1957/58, the latter of which saw the Hoops beat Rangers 7–1 in the final – undoubtedly McGrory's finest hour-and-a-half as Celtic manager. And, in 1953, his side also won the Coronation Cup unexpectedly.

He was replaced by Jock Stein in 1965, becoming the club's Public Relations Office, though Stein would always insist that everyone refer to McGrory as 'Boss'. He respected McGrory's achievements as a player and, having worked under him in the 1950s, understood the environment that the manager was working in at that time.

It was also a mark of respect from one great man to another and McGrory, ever the gentleman and a true Celtic man, appreciated the gesture and enjoyed the success his former player brought to the club as much as any supporter.

AND ANOTHER THING ...

He scored 468 goals for Celtic and if you'd cut him, Jimmy McGrory would probably have bled green and white. The boy from the Garngad would have dreamt about becoming a Bhoy, and he would also have known how important it was to beat Rangers, by now Celtic's main rivals and in the post-First World War years a club which had formed a blinkered signing policy that excluded Catholics, which extended for much of the twentieth century.

Yet, of those 468 goals, only thirteen came against Rangers. The first two came in a 5–0 thrashing of the Ibrox club in the 1925 Scottish Cup semi-final, while his final strike against Celtic's city rivals was also part of a double, on 1 January 1936 when the Hoops lost 4–3 at Celtic Park.

The breakdown of his goals against opposing teams is as follows: Hamilton Academical (28); Queen's Park (26); Falkirk (24); Motherwell (23); Kilmarnock (22); Cowdenbeath (22); Dunfermline (22); Third Lanark (21); St Mirren (19); Hibernian (18); Aberdeen (18); Hearts (17); Airdrie (17); St Johnstone (16); Partick Thistle (16); Clyde (16); Dundee (14); Morton (14); Ayr United (14); Rangers (13); Arbroath (10); Leith Athletic (10); Dundee United (9); Queen of the South (9); East Fife (7); Albion Rovers (7); Raith Rovers (7); Brechin City (4); Bo'ness (4); Alloa Athletic (3); Keith (3); Arthurlie (3); Stenhousemuir (3); Clydebank (2); Dumbarton (2); East Stirling (2); Inverness Caledonian (2); Solway Star (1).

Not surprisingly, Jimmy McGrory was a favourite amongst Celtic supporters, and for those lucky enough to have seen him play, it was a memory which never left them.

Cardinal Thomas Winning, the leader of the Roman Catholic Church in Scotland, speaking in June 2001 shortly before his untimely death, identified the striker as his favourite player from childhood. 'There was a great song at that time to the tune of Hail Glorious St Patrick about McGrory,' explained Cardinal Winning, before breaking into song:

> In the war against Rangers, in the fight for the cup,
> Wee Jimmy McGrory put Celtic five up.
> He did it before and he'll do it again.
> Wee Jimmy McGrory, the pride of Parkhead.

'You were very tempted to sing that in Church on the feast of St Patrick because it came more readily to the lips,' the Cardinal said.

He cheered him as a player, supported the team that McGrory managed and later, as Archbishop of Glasgow, he officiated at the Celtic legend's funeral in 1982.

2

BOBBY LENNOX

273 GOALS IN 571 APPEARANCES

The problem with many of the great Celtic strikers from history is that very few people of different generations were able to witness them in action. Not all of the players who have scored over 100 goals for the club enjoyed the sort of longevity that the three Jimmys – McMenemy, McGrory and Quinn – managed. Bobby Lennox is one who did. The revered Lisbon Lion made his debut in 1962 and was still going strong in 1980. It is simply remarkable to think that he scored for Celtic in three separate decades, enabling so many Celtic supporters to witness his talents.

What makes Lennox's ongoing relevance to the Celtic teams of the 1960s, '70s and '80s even more impressive is the success he achieved during his glittering career with the club. In Scotland, he won the lot and then won them again and again. In the European arena, he was a vital component of Jock Stein's 1967 side that brought the big cup back to Celtic Park. Lennox boasted searing pace, intelligence, balance and a deadly eye for goal and would have graced any side in the world when he was on song. His record of 273 goals in 571 appearances suggests that was more often than not.

The only member of the Lisbon Lions to be born outwith the Greater Glasgow area, Bobby, who hailed from Saltcoats, entered the world on 30 August 1943, and showed an immediate talent for the game as he wreaked havoc in the Ayrshire youth leagues.

11

He joined Celtic in September 1961 and emerged as a potent weapon for the club. By the time he had finished his playing career, Bobby possessed 11 championship medals, eight Scottish Cup medals and four League Cup medals. His most treasured possession remains the European Cup gong from 1967.

Jimmy McGrory is the only man to have scored more goals for Celtic than Bobby. In the modern age, when players change clubs more frequently, it's hard to envisage these records ever being broken. It's fitting that they sit together at the top of the scoring charts. They were both great Celtic servants and wonderful players for the club. Lennox was a different type of player from McGrory but played an equally important role in the club's history. In fact, given that, in 2002, he was voted into the club's greatest ever team ahead of McGrory, many would argue that Lennox is even more important.

As Lennox mingles happily with supporters in his current role as a match-day host at Celtic Park, you would never realise you were in the presence of Celtic royalty. Bobby was Celtic's special weapon. He was a jet-heeled striker with dynamite in his boots. Give him a chance and he would take it. Bobby Lennox will forever be regarded as one of the most decorated players in Celtic's history. Billy McNeill, who played with Lennox and managed him, summed his status up when he said: 'Bobby knows what it means to pull on a Celtic jersey.'

FIRST GOAL

Growing up, Bobby Lennox had simple aims. He wanted to be either a motor mechanic or a footballer. As he entered his teenage years, he didn't know which vocation he would follow, but as the years flew past and his football talent started causing interest in his native Saltcoats, Lennox hoped he would one day become a professional. Not that he got everything handed to him on a plate; the young Lennox was playing local football and working in a gargantuan ICI plant when Celtic came calling. 'I worked in the box factory and it was my job to make hundreds of boxes every day.' He had known all about earning a living the hard way.

Professional football was more to his taste, but it wasn't going to be easy for Lennox to cope with the step up. He was full of speed and incisive runs, but at 5ft 8in he wasn't the biggest. Defenders would be more physical in the senior game, but Lennox went on to prove he had the intelligence to match his pace and shooting ability as he turned into a goal machine for Celtic.

Yet, while his pace was explosive, Bobby didn't exactly burst on to the scene. He made his Celtic debut against Dundee in March 1962 but that was his only appearance of the season. In the following campaign, he made nine appearances but had yet to break his duck. 1963/64 saw Lennox feature just eight times in total, but the goals started to flow. His first came against Third Lanark in a 4–4 draw on 14 September, while just three days later he was again on target as Celtic beat Basel 5–1 in the first round of the Cup-Winners' Cup.

From Lennox, this was a sure sign of what was to come. In 1964/65, he scored sixteen times in thirty-seven games and never looked back. Successive 25-goal hauls helped Celtic dominate Scottish football and he broke through the 100-mark with 41 strikes in 1967/68. He continued to hammer home the goals for the remainder of his career and Bobby would go on to score 273 goals in total. It's a staggering tally that includes fifteen hat-tricks for the club. Only Jimmy McGrory and Jimmy Quinn have scored more trebles.

100TH GOAL

Bobby Lennox was always one of the top strikers in Britain during the halcyon days of Celtic's glorious run under Jock Stein, but in terms of goals, the striker's best season came in 1967/68 when he topped the club's scoring charts with forty-one. What makes this tally even more impressive is that Celtic were knocked out of both the Scottish Cup and European Cup at the first stage. Of Bobby's forty-one goals that season, thirty-two came in the league, seven were scored in the League Cup and he netted in each tie against Dynamo Kiev as Celtic went out 3–2 on aggregate in Europe.

There was also a milestone in that season for Bobby as he scored his 100th goal for the club. It came in the midst of a phenomenal scoring run for Lennox, who grabbed an incredible twenty goals in his last twelve league games of the 1967/68 campaign. He could do no wrong as Celtic pulled off another championship win and his 100th goal came against Aberdeen in a 1–0 win at Pittodrie on 10 April 1968. He was on the hottest streak of his Celtic career.

What was a typical Lennox goal? There was no such thing. They came in all different shapes and sizes, but he was at his best playing on the shoulder of the last defender and timing his run to perfection as he beat the offside trap. Indeed, while happy with his official tally of 273 Celtic goals, he often wonders how many it could have been had he not been serially halted by dodgy offside decisions. Lennox once had three goals chalked off against Dundee United and also famously had a strike against Liverpool controversially ruled out in the 1965/66 Cup-Winners' Cup semi-final. He says:

There were a few offside decisions that went against me that I still look back on. There are certain goals I can see

14

clearly and know that when Bobby Murdoch or Bertie Auld made the pass, I was never offside. Sometimes I could even see the linesman looking up and by that time I was already by someone. Put it this way, I know I should have a few extra goals to my credit. I just had to keep going in there though, making the runs and not letting my head go down. I would get annoyed from time to time, but there was nothing I could do about it.

LAST GOAL

Compared with 1962, the football world of 1980 seemed light years away. Tactics were different, equipment was different, boots were different ... everything had changed. In the Celtic first-team squad, however, there was one constant and that was Bobby Lennox. 12 April 1980 was the date of his last goal for Celtic and it came in a 5–0 Scottish Cup semi-final win over Hibernian.

Lennox enjoyed an Indian summer that season. He was in his late thirties but Billy McNeill valued his experience and ability. He had left Celtic for Houston Hurricane in March 1978 but was tempted home six months later. In 1979/80, George McCluskey, who would score the winner in the Scottish Cup final against Rangers to give Lennox his last medal for Celtic, was the club's main striker, but Lennox played a vital role. He made thirty-one starts, played forty-seven times in total and bagged ten goals for Celtic that season. Some eighteen years after signing for the club, Lennox was still operating at the highest level.

Victory over Rangers gave Bobby his eighth and final Scottish Cup medal for Celtic and continued his affinity with the competition. He played in 1965 when Jock Stein's men started a period of dominance and was in the side that beat Aberdeen in 1967. Lennox scored as Rangers were humiliated in a 4–0 victory in

1969 and was also on target as Aberdeen inflicted a 3–1 defeat on Celtic in 1970. Bobby won further medals in 1971, 1972, 1974 and 1975, as well as 1980, although he was an unused substitute in 1972 and 1974.

The League Cup wasn't quite as kind to Lennox but he still picked up four winner's medals in 1965, 1966, 1967 and 1968. He scored the only goal of the game in 1966 as Celtic beat Rangers 1–0 to start the Lisbon season in the best possible fashion and followed that up with a goal in the 1967, 5–3 final win over Dundee. Just twelve months later, he scored a hat-trick as Celtic beat Hibernian 6–2 in the 1968 League Cup final.

Life after Celtic's first team was a life coaching Celtic's youngsters for Bobby, who was appointed on to the backroom staff and spent many years taking the club's reserve side before leaving in 1993. It's still phenomenal to think that, barring those six months in America, Bobby never represented any another senior football side apart from Celtic. While not officially a one-club man, he deserves to be regarded as one. Celtic has always been Bobby's one true football love. He said recently:

I am a Celtic supporter as everybody knows and it's great to have had such a long association with the club. It's a privilege that I really appreciate. It's been a great honour and I enjoyed so many good times with the club, not just as a player and a supporter, but off the park as well. I have made great friends; The Lisbon Lions are like brothers. I have been lucky enough to play in two or three different teams, with players like Roy Aitken, Danny McGrain, Kenny Dalglish, George McCluskey and Davie Provan, I have been fortunate enough to have played with loads of good players and in four completely different Celtic teams. I have been really fortunate.

HIGHS AND LOWS

Ask Bobby Lennox to list the highs of his Celtic career and he will be there all day. That's not down to arrogance or an egotistical nature, it's simply because he achieved so much in such a long period of time at the club. Ask him for highlights and he will think of signing for Celtic, of the 1965 Scottish Cup final, of Lisbon, of one of his many goals against Rangers, of ten men winning the league in 1979 and championship medal after championship medal. These days, he is a keen golfer but he was never happier than when he was scoring goals wearing a Celtic strip.

'I have so many highlights from my career that I couldn't pick out one,' says Lennox.

There was my first ever goal against Rangers, the final whistle in Lisbon, even the final whistle in the semi-final of the European Cup that year. There was also my goal against Read Madrid when we beat them 1–0 in Alfredo Di Stefano's testimonial. There was the League Cup final where I scored and we beat Rangers 1–0. There was also the final whistle in our first cup win against Dunfermline in 1965 and the time when I was made captain for six weeks in 1975. Everybody knew that Kenny Dalglish was going to be captain in the long-term, but they made me acting captain for six weeks and that was a great honour.

Playing as long as I did was also a great achievement. I think that I was the only guy who played every year that Jock was manager. I don't want to sound big-headed in saying that, but I thought he was the greatest manager ever and for him to pick me was a genuine honour. To have scored for Celtic in the 1960s, 1970s and 1980s is something else that I am quite pleased with.

Every single one of Lennox's Celtic honours – his eleven league titles, eight Scottish Cups and four League Cups – act as highlights. But one feat always outweighs the others and for Lennox that was in Lisbon when Celtic won the European Cup in 1967. He never scored in the 2–1 win over Inter Milan but played his part like the entire Celtic squad did that season, scoring twice on the run to the final.

Celtic's win in Lisbon saw them qualify for the World Club Championship against Racing Club, but what should have been one of the proudest events in the club's history turned into one of the most infamous as the dirty tactics of the Argentines saw a play-off in Uruguay turn into a battle, with Lennox sent off for no reason. After home and away legs, the score was 2–2 and a bad-tempered play-off ensued. Lennox said:

> They tried to kick us off the park in both legs, but we thought we would beat them in the play-off. I wanted to play, but I only lasted twenty minutes. It was farcical. The referee had actually stopped the game and told Billy McNeill that at the next incident he was sending off our number eight and their number six. Big Billy shouted to me and said, 'Bobby, the next incident and you're off.' I just couldn't believe it. I don't know whether that was part of the plan over there, but I was off right away. Then Jimmy Johnstone got sent off and so did Bertie Auld but he refused to go. Only Bertie could have done that and got away with it.

Racing Club won that match 1–0 and there was further heartache to come for Lennox when Celtic lost 2—1 to Feyenoord in the 1970 European Cup final. Quite simply, it was the worst moment of his entire career. 'That was the lowest point,' he says.

It is the one regret I have from my time at Celtic and I still think about it today. We could have been double European champions, two-time winners. We didn't play well on the night, even though everybody had us as big favourites. Guys who have been in that situation and lost will know what I am talking about – the European Cup final is one of the biggest games you could lose. I still don't like thinking about it.

AND ANOTHER THING ...

Bobby Lennox's favourite Celtic game came when he scored a hat-trick against Rangers in a Glasgow Cup match, but those goals are not counted in his overall tally for the club. Only goals scored in the Scottish League, Scottish Cup, League Cup and Europe are deemed official strikes. Regardless, it was a supreme performance from Bobby, as he grabbed three and Billy McNeill scored the other in a rout. 'That game included my best goal against Rangers,' said Lennox. 'I was played in through the inside-right position, cut inside John Greig and hit it in off the underside of the bar. I was really pleased with that one.'

Like so many of his Celtic teammates, Lennox never got the international recognition he deserved, with his overall total of just ten caps being a scandalous example of the Scotland selection policy. He did, however, score in the famous 3–2 win over England at Wembley in 1967, when Scotland beat the reigning world champions. In 2008, he was also inducted into the SFA Hall of Fame and said:

I was thrilled when I was picked and that comes from when you look who is in it. It's unbelievable, being compared to all these guys and it's even more amazing when you think who isn't in it. It's a great honour.

19

Manchester United and England legend Bobby Charlton regards Lennox as one of the best strikers in the history of the game. He played alongside him as a Celtic guest in a testimonial for Liverpool defender Ron Yeats in 1974, and struck up an immediate partnership with him. Charlton later said: 'If I'd had Bobby Lennox in my team, I could have played forever. All I had to do was look up and pick out his run. He was one of the best strikers I've ever seen.'

Bobby had two nicknames during his playing days. He was often referred to as the 'Buzzbomb' because of his blistering pace, while his more common nickname was 'Lemon', which he still answers to today. Many stories have been told about the origins of that particular moniker, but the true background is that Willie Wallace spotted the name 'Lemon' in a Celtic match report in a newspaper. There had obviously been a mix-up but the name stuck.

3

HENRIK LARSSON

242 GOALS IN 315 GAMES

Henrik Larsson is a man who was always destined for football greatness, yet took slightly longer than most of his contemporaries to fully realise his potential. By the age of twenty-one, Larsson was still playing part-time football before an offer to sign with his local semi-professional club, Helsingborgs IF, changed his life. An instant hit in the Swedish lower leagues, the dreadlocked Larsson, whose father hailed from the Cape Verde islands and mother came from Sweden, helped Helsingborgs into the top tier for the first time in twenty-two years and was rewarded with a move to Dutch giants Feyenoord in 1993.

He did enough in his first season in Holland to earn a slot in the Swedish World Cup squad in 1994 and helped his country to a third-place finish in America. Larsson would go on to represent Sweden in the 2002 and 2006 World Cups, as well as the 2000, 2004 and 2008 European Championships. While his international feats earned him the prestigious honour of being named, in 2005, as the best Swedish player of the last fifty years, Larsson's club achievements stand alongside those of any of his peers.

After four years with Feyenoord, he swapped Holland for Scotland in 1997 when he followed mentor Wim Jansen to be part of his Celtic revolution. It turned out to be a protracted transfer, with a Dutch tribunal finally setting a fee of £650,000 after a long-running dispute between the player and his club. It proved to one of the biggest bargains in football history.

Jansen won the league in his historic first season in Glasgow, which also turned out to be his last campaign after he departed days after the season's denouement. Larsson could have followed him, yet opted to stay for the long haul, even when Manchester United came knocking in 1999. Loyalty was always one of his best attributes.

It was a match made in heaven. Larsson was good for Celtic, while Celtic were undoubtedly good for him as well. He was paid handsomely during his seven years but proved his worth with the staggering total of 242 goals in 315 appearances. Had it not been for a horrific leg break in 1999, that tally would have been higher.

In terms of silverware, he picked up four SPL titles, two Scottish Cups and two League Cups. On the European front, he naturally proved prolific and set a British goal record during his seven years at Celtic. He also won the European Golden Boot in 2001 and helped Celtic reach the UEFA Cup final in 2003.

After extending his contract in the early years of the twenty-first century, Larsson announced he would be leaving Celtic when his deal expired in 2004. His initial plan was to head home to Helsingborgs and Sweden. Despite attempts to keep him at Celtic, he stayed true to his word and bowed out before Euro 2004, hinting that he wanted to leave before he was past his best. At the time, few observers doubted that he could carry on for at least three more years and Larsson's subsequent career, post-Celtic, backed up that theory. After a productive Euro 2004 for Sweden, Larsson joined Barcelona. Injury hindered his debut season at the Nou Camp, yet the Swede battled back and played an integral role in the Catalan side's 2006 Champions League triumph, setting up two goals in the 2–1 final win over Arsenal.

Thierry Henry, then of Arsenal, displayed rare humility as he paid tribute to Larsson, moments after the final whistle: 'You need to talk about the proper footballer who made the difference for Barcelona and that was Henrik Larsson tonight,' he said.

Brazilian Ronaldinho, a teammate of Larsson's at Barcelona and the best player in the world at that point, was equally effusive in his praise of the striker: 'Henrik was my idol even before he came to Barcelona. I remember him playing for Sweden in the 1994 World Cup. Henrik taught me a lot about football and I learned even more from him as a person.'

Finally, two years after leaving Celtic, Larsson returned to where it all started at Helsingborgs in 2006 and remained there until he retired in 2009. Yet, there was a final twist in his incredible story as he accepted the invitation to join Manchester United on loan in January 2007. He spent three months at Old Trafford and captured the hearts the United faithful. Alex Ferguson, who had tried to sign Larsson during the early days of his Celtic career, could only admire the talents of a true great.

Now beginning a managerial career in Sweden, Henrik Larsson has had a wondrous career in football. He deserves to be classed among the modern greats of the game, yet has never forgotten where it really all started for him.

'Celtic is my club,' he said in May 2008.

I've played with a few teams, but I made myself as a player at Celtic. I'll be eternally grateful to Celtic because they took a chance on me when other clubs didn't. It was there where I became recognised as a player. It was there that I went on to play in European Championships and World Cups with Sweden. The club believed in me and I'll always remember that.

FIRST GOAL

As Darren Collier bent down to pick up the size five Mitre nestling in the net, he probably felt like the loneliest man in the world. Seven years later, more than a few goalkeepers would know that feeling well. Collier is the Englishman who holds the distinction of being the first goalkeeper to be beaten by Henrik Larsson during the Swede's Celtic career. If it's any consolation, he finds himself in the best of company now.

The date of Larsson's first Celtic goal was 9 August 1997. The venue was Tynecastle Stadium in Edinburgh. Celtic's opponents were Berwick Rangers in a second-round League Cup match. Only 6,267 supporters were there to witness that historic moment. For a man who specialised in the spectacular during his seven years in Scotland, there is something slightly mundane about Larsson's first goal for Celtic. Yet, even the most memorable adventures start with a small step and for the Swede that came in the 7–0 trouncing of Berwick.

The strike itself was gloriously simple in its execution. Craig Burley fired a free kick to the back post, Malky Mackay rose above the Berwick defence and nodded back across goal for Larsson, who fired home from close range. There was no 'Henrik's tongue' or the aeroplane celebration that became his trademark in the ensuing years. Instead, there were a few muted high fives. Most importantly, Larsson's Celtic career was off and running.

Desperate to join up with Wim Jansen at Celtic in the summer of 1997, Larsson found himself embroiled in a legal wrangle with Feyenoord. The Swede and his agent, Rob Jansen, claimed there was a clause in his contract stipulating that the player could leave for a fee in the region of £600,000. The Dutch side protested and Larsson, out of the Feyenoord side at that point, was left in limbo. Finally, a tribunal panel voted in Larsson's favour and he was off to Glasgow after an emotionally draining period in his life. Some of that frustration was taken out on Berwick Rangers.

Not that the Tynecastle contest was the first time Celtic fans had clapped eyes on Larsson. Six days earlier, the Swede had made his debut against Hibernian in the opening league match of the season at Easter Road. Named as a substitute, Larsson came on for Andreas Thom just before the hour-mark. He was desperate to make an impact and did so – only at the wrong end. Picking up a loose ball at the edge of the box, his attempted pass was intercepted by Chic Charnley. In an instant, the ball was in the bottom corner and Celtic had lost 2–1.

First impressions can be deceiving and Larsson soon showed his class. Prior to joining, most Celtic supporters only knew him as the dreadlocked, willowy wide player who featured for Sweden at World Cup 1994 with varying success. Yet, Larsson was an entirely different proposition three years later. His spell with Feyenoord in Holland had made him stronger and Wim Jansen had successfully moulded him into a central striker. 'For me, Henrik was the perfect professional,' was Jansen's view.

At Celtic, Larsson would play up front, or just off the main striker. He was initially hailed as a replacement for the maverick playmaker Paolo Di Canio, but in terms of teamwork and self-lessness, Larsson was streets ahead and proved a perfect foil for Simon Donnelly and Harald Brattbakk. After his first strike against Berwick, Larsson settled and weighed in with some monumental goals as Celtic won the League Cup and clinched the Scottish Premier League title for the first time in ten years, stopping Rangers' bid for ten-in-a-row in the process.

Highlights from Larsson's 19-goal debut season include his effort against Dundee United in the 3–0 League Cup final and his scorching drive against St Johnstone on the day the league title was won. So, from Berwick's Darren Collier to St Johnstone's Alan Main, goalkeepers across Scotland were left cursing Henrik

Larsson. It had been an impressive first season, but there would be much more to come.

100TH GOAL

Such was the prolific scoring rate of Henrik Larsson, it soon became a matter of when, and not if, he would reach the 100-goal mark for Celtic. He had emerged as a bona fide goal machine. Number fifty had arrived when he hit four against Motherwell in a 7–1 Fir Park victory in February 1999. Injury meant the next milestone would be reached just less than two years later, but you always knew it would be a memorable occasion.

True to form, the Swede did it in spectacular style with another four-goal haul against Kilmarnock on 2 January 2001, which accounted for numbers 98, 99, 100 and 101 in his Celtic career. On reflection, Larsson probably knew he was on the verge of making history that day and decided he wouldn't stop until he did so. Or maybe he just liked scoring against Kilmarnock.

Certainly the facts back up that last theory. During that particular campaign, Larsson plundered eight goals against Killie, including a further hat-trick in the 3–0 CIS Cup final victory at Hampden in March. He would return to the National Stadium in May 2001 to round off an exceptional season with two goals in the 3–0 Scottish Cup final win against Hibernian. This clinched Celtic's first domestic treble since 1969.

Season 2000/01 was Larsson's own *annus mirabilis*. Put simply, everything he touched turned to gold as the arrival of Martin O'Neill as manager coincided with the Swede hitting the form of his life.

Having missed the bulk of the previous campaign through injury, Larsson returned fitter than ever after starring for Sweden in Euro 2000. O'Neill, quickly realising his world-class talent, built his side around the striker. 'A great player is a great player in whatever era,' said O'Neill of Larsson in 2004. 'I think the fact that Henrik came to Celtic and took his place in Celtic's history is magical in itself. He deserves his place in the order of merit at Celtic.'

Fittingly, the first competitive goal of O'Neill's reign came via the left foot of Larsson. Dundee United were the opponents and Chris Sutton's second goal secured a 2–1 win. This would be a sign of things to come. Larsson and Sutton were a partnership to rank alongside any in Celtic's history. Combining grace, power and pace, they scored a collective total of sixty-seven goals in their debut season. 'Henrik is the best all-round player that I have ever played with,' was Sutton's verdict of the Swede. 'There is no edge or arrogance to him. On the pitch, he's the most unselfish player I've ever worked with.'

Larsson, however, was still the undisputed star of one of the most revered teams in Celtic's history. By January, when he reached the 100-mark, he had scored 33 goals in all competitions. One of those will go down as the greatest of Larsson's Celtic career. It came in the 6–2 win over Rangers at Celtic Park and saw the Swede nonchalantly chip Stefan Klos for a goal of supreme quality.

Not that he liked the limelight. His mantra at press conferences became, 'It's not about me, it's about the team,' even when he was shattering records all across Europe. 'What I achieved that season was all down to the team,' he later reflected. 'The way we played gave me the chance to score goals.'

Including international games, Larsson finished that campaign with a staggering fifty-eight goals. That tally would be enough to earn Larsson the European Golden Boot, to sit alongside the three medals he'd won for Celtic – he even hit a hole-in-one at Tom Boyd's Testimonial golf day. He was playing at the peak of his powers ... or was he? The Henrik Larsson Celtic story still had plenty of mileage. And to just to show he really meant business, the dreadlocks had gone as well.

LAST GOAL

The familiar terrace anthem echoed around Hampden Park as the Celtic team embarked on a lap of honour after bagging yet another piece of silverware. Only this time, the tone of the singing was different. It was more poignant. As the strains of 'You are my Larsson' died down, the stark reality of the occasion must have dawned on Celtic supporters of all ages. The Larsson era was over. They were bidding farewell to an icon; a true phenomenon.

While a friendly match against Seville, billed as Henrik's 'Farewell Fiesta', would allow the Celtic support to extend their gratitude to Larsson within the confines of Celtic Park, Larsson's goodbye in a competitive environment came on 22 May 2004. In some ways, you couldn't help but feel sorry for Dunfermline, Celtic's opponents in that Scottish Cup final. They had fought hard to reach Hampden, but were never going to triumph in a match that was a celebration of Larsson's incredible seven-year contribution to Celtic Football Club.

In fairness, Dunfermline did have their moments during the emotional ninety minutes. Andrius Skerla's freak opener saw Celtic trail at the interval and Larsson's inevitable intervention was delayed until the fifty-eighth minute. When Jackie McNamara drilled a long clearance up-field, he probably envisaged Larsson hustling Dunfermline's Aaron Labonte for a few seconds, to allow Celtic to move up-field.

Yet, the Swede had made a career out of pulling off the extraordinary and wasn't in the mood to stop in his last competitive game for Celtic. He pick-pocketed the Dunfermline defender, raced away and curled an exquisite shot into the corner. It was 1–1 at that point and Larsson still had unfinished business to contend with. As the game entered its final quarter, he struck again. Accepting Neil Lennon's pass, he rolled his marker, Labonte, and placed a left-foot shot into the bottom corner for goal number 242.

The Larsson Final had, unsurprisingly, lived up to its moniker. Stilian Petrov added a third for Celtic to kill off Dunfermline's challenge, but the day belonged to Larsson.

In addition to his incredible record in front of goal, Larsson's value has never been underestimated by his teammates, wherever he has played his football. Welsh striker John Hartson, who often partnered Larsson at Celtic, said of the Swede. 'He was very unselfish. If he thought you were in a better position, he would pass to you. He was very much a team player and that's unusual for a guy who scored so many goals.'

Just seven days earlier, the striker had also made the most of another emotional occasion; this time his last competitive game for Celtic at Celtic Park. Tears flowed that day as the Swedish master finished his SPL career with a double in the 2–1 win over Dundee United at Celtic Park. With the league title clinched, the match was relatively meaningless, but Celtic supporters arrived from all over the world to witness the scenes on another emotional day.

'When I scored in that Dundee United game it hit me straight away that it was the final time playing for Celtic in a competitive game at Celtic Park and that was an amazing day for me,' said Larsson.

It was unbelievable, the whole thing. It is something I could never have dreamt of when I came here in 1997 and signed my contract. There are not many players who have had the chance to experience what I have at Celtic. I feel very privileged.

Larsson, never a man to show his emotions, broke down in tears at the end of that match as his teammates formed a guard of honour and the crowd, to a man, gave a standing ovation to the King of Kings.

HIGHS AND LOWS

Henrik Larsson scored 242 goals in 315 matches for Celtic over 7 seasons. He won 4 SPL titles, 2 League Cups, 2 Scottish Cups and also played in the 2003 UEFA Cup final. After taking all that into consideration, it's perhaps obvious that the highs far outweigh the lows of Larsson's Celtic career. Yet, the lowest point is arguably one of the most important moments of the club's modern history.

Lying flat on his back inside the Stade Gerland in Lyon, his shattered leg hanging limply, Larsson feared for his career. It was 21 October 1999, and he wouldn't kick a competitive ball until the last game of that season, in May 2000. Without his immeasurable influence, Celtic imploded. John Barnes, the rookie manager, had only been in charge for four months when Larsson suffered that horrific injury. Robbed of his talisman, he would be out of a job by early February.

The impact the loss of Larsson had on Barnes' tenure cannot be underestimated. Playing beside Mark Viduka, the Swede had scored thirteen goals in the opening three months of the campaign as Barnes' Celtic picked up a maximum twenty-four points from their first eight games. With Larsson undergoing his rehab, Celtic stuttered badly and Barnes' position became untenable when Inverness Caledonian Thistle left Celtic Park with a 3–1 win the Scottish Cup. It was the nadir of a difficult season.

Had Larsson been fit, it's impossible to imagine that terminal situation developing. His goals were crucial to Barnes, as they were to every manager he played under, and Larsson's injury signalled the beginning of the end for the Englishman.

Yet, every cloud has a silver lining. With Barnes gone, Celtic were forced to look for another manager and Martin O'Neill arrived in 2000. Domestic dominance ensued with three titles in five years.

Following O'Neill's departure and Gordon Strachan's arrival, a further three SPL titles had been won, while the proud European record enjoyed by the Irishman had also been carried on, with Celtic regularly competing in the last sixteen of the Champions League. In hindsight, it can be argued that Larsson's injury did more to shape Celtic's success in the first decade of the new Millennium than anything else. Had Larsson stayed fit and Barnes remained in charge, success may well have been attained. But would it have been on the same scale, both domestically and in Europe?

Certainly, the arrival of O'Neill proved ideal for Larsson and allowed him to enjoy highs he could never have imagined. When O'Neill swept into power, Larsson already had an SPL gong, won in dramatic circumstances in 1998, and a League Cup medal to his name, but the Irishman took Celtic and the Swede to a new level.

In four trophy-laden years under the Irish manager, Larsson won three league titles, one League Cup and two Scottish Cups. He topped the scoring charts in every season and scooped a host of personal awards, including that prestigious European Golden Boot.

Larsson also prospered on the European scene under O'Neill, who led Celtic into the group stages of the Champions League for the first time in 2001, and also guided the club to the UEFA Cup final in 2003. Derided by some clueless football 'experts' as a player who could only score in the SPL, Larsson duly prospered on every stage, with his thirty-five goals for Celtic in

European competition a record amount for a player with a British club.

'The hallmark of any great player is the fact that they score at the top level and Henrik has done that in both European and domestic football,' said O'Neill, speaking in 2004. 'He is simply a natural goalscorer.'

Larsson's best individual performance as a Celtic player arguably came in the UEFA Cup final when he scored twice in the 3–2 defeat by FC Porto. Despite the loss, he was the King of Spain in the eyes of the Celtic supporters that night. Larsson though, didn't even attempt to hide his disappointment. 'I didn't see anything positive about my performance in the final,' was his reaction. 'Scoring two goals in a final doesn't mean anything if you lose. All I wanted was for Celtic to win the UEFA Cup.'

AND ANOTHER THING ...

Strangely, for a man with such a prolific record for Celtic, Henrik Larsson's first and last competitive goals at Celtic Park were actually both against Celtic. He scored an own goal in an epic UEFA Cup match against Tirol Innsbruck on 26 August 1997, and then returned to Celtic Park in 2004 with Barcelona, scoring the clinching goal in a 3–1 win for the Catalans.

He was always a man for the big occasion, especially cup finals. During his Celtic career, Larsson played in eight finals and scored eleven goals. He also scored as Celtic clinched the title in 1998 and hit a hat-trick as the Hoops beat Livingston to become champions in 2002.

Up to May 2010, Larsson had appeared in more Celtic Huddles than any other player; a total of 312 during his time in Glasgow. Only Jackie McNamara and Neil Lennon come close to that record with 307 and 300 respectively. He played under a total of five managers during his time at Celtic: Wim Jansen (1997–1998), Dr Jozef Venglos (1998–1999), John Barnes (1999–2000) Kenny Dalglish (2000) and Martin O'Neill (2000–2004).

Due to his time in Scotland, he was awarded an honorary degree from the University of Strathclyde for his contribution to sport and charity work. He was also awarded the King's Medal in Sweden in 2007.

4

STEVIE CHALMERS

231 GOALS IN 406 APPEARANCES

Stevie Chalmers scored the most important goal in Celtic history. That's a statement that looks unlikely to change for the foreseeable future. So when one goal you've scored can be heralded in such grandiose terms, then do the other 230 pale into insignificance?

There's no point pretending that any of Stevie Chalmers' other goals are remembered as fondly, or revered as fervently, as the one he scored in Lisbon on 25 May 1967. That was the goal which won the European Cup for Celtic.

They became the first British club to do so, and for a team which had only won its first league title in twelve years the season before, it represented one of the most remarkable transformations of a football team ever seen.

Orchestrated by Jock Stein, the legend of the Lisbon Lions was born in Portugal that day as eleven men all born within a thirty-mile radius of Celtic Park became the Champions of Europe.

Tommy Gemmell scored the equaliser after Inter Milan had taken the lead through a first-half penalty – and Gemmell can boast of having scored in two European finals, thanks to his strike three years later against Feyenoord in Milan – but it was the boot of Chalmers which steered Bobby Murdoch's shot into the back of the Inter net with just five minutes of the match remaining to give Celtic a 2–1 victory and ensure immortality for the players and their manager.

The player himself will not complain that he is remembered for this one moment as opposed to the goals he scored in a twelve-year period at the club which would make him the fourth top goalscorer in Celtic's history, behind only Henrik Larsson (242), his friend and teammate Bobby Lennox (273), and the peerless Jimmy McGrory (468). After all, how many strikers get to score such a significant goal?

Chalmers said:

The highlight of my Celtic career has to be scoring the winning goal against Inter Milan in the European Cup final. I don't think you can get a better highlight than that. You work every day from when you're a kid, building yourself up to that kind of challenge and it was something I had dreamed of.

I am very, very lucky and I have a lot of other highlights that I can pick out as well. Just signing for Celtic was one of the greatest days in my career and there were a lot of clubs interested in signing. The second that Celtic declared their interest, the other clubs were forgotten. It was a dream to play for Celtic

I can still picture my goal in Lisbon – I remember it as clear as day. That occasion will never fade in my memory and for every player who was in the team and involved in that squad, it was a tremendous achievement. A lot of people thought that we were going there just to make up the numbers, but to go there and win, and win in the commanding style that we did win, was something to be proud of.

Yet, Stevie Chalmers should also be remembered for those other 230 goals as well because they point to the fact that he was a truly great goalscorer. He arrived at a club in the doldrums, where regular success was a fading pre-war memory and he left when they were the dominant force in Scotland and one of the best teams in Europe.

There were a number of factors for that, the most important of which was the appointment of Jock Stein as manager, but Chalmers' goals played a contributory part as well.

The Lisbon Lions can boast of five Century Bhoys in their ranks – Lennox, Johnstone, Murdoch and Wallace joining Chalmers – and that's compelling evidence of the type of team Celtic were in that period; while John Hughes, who didn't play in that final, also chalked up a superb total of 188 goals. Consider too that, but for the serious knee injury he sustained in December 1966, Joe McBride would also be among this select group of players, and probably up near the top of the scoring charts.

Stevie Chalmers scored 231 goals in 406 appearances for Celtic, and that is a remarkable record. There were vital goals against Rangers, doubles, trebles and even a couple of fives thrown in for good measure.

But there will always be one goal that is spoken about before all others, and Stevie Chalmers wouldn't have it any other way.

FIRST GOAL

Stevie Chalmers joined Celtic in February 1959 at the age of twenty-two, having spent the previous three years at junior side Ashfield after he'd completed National Service. His debut came in March of that year, in a 2–1 defeat against Airdrie at Celtic Park in a season when Celtic finished sixth in the league. It was also just a year after the great 7–1 League Cup final triumph over Rangers, but the club appeared to be settling back into a period of underachievement.

That was Chalmers' only appearance for the season, though

he would enjoy a greater involvement with the first team the following year, when he also scored his first goal for the club.

That came on 19 September 1959, in an away league game against Raith Rovers. Celtic were comfortable 3–0 winners that day, and after Mike Jackson had given the Hoops the lead, Chalmers weighed in with two second-half goals, the first of them coming on fifty-one minutes to get his tally up and running.

He scored fifteen goals that season, one less than John Divers, but seven behind the club's top goalscorer, Neilly Mochan.

Blessed with tremendous pace, Chalmers was an asset to the team but it was only with the arrival of Jock Stein that his strengths were harnessed properly for the good of the team.

However, that's not to underestimate what he contributed to the team prior to Stein's appointment. In 1960/61, he was top goalscorer with twenty-six goals in all competitions, though once again it was a barren season for Celtic, who lost 2–0 in a Scottish Cup final replay to Dunfermline Athletic, who were managed by none other than Jock Stein.

The former defender, Stein, had actually been at Celtic Park as reserve team coach since 1957, when his training methods were already impressing his young charges, but he was keen to forge a career as a manager in his own right and Dunfermline gave him his first opportunity. He repaid them by delivering the Scottish Cup in his first season in charge.

That season saw some significant departures from Celtic, with Neilly Mochan joining Dundee United and Bertie Auld being sold to Birmingham City, while Willie Fernie returned from Middlesbrough for a brief spell. The club felt his experience would be beneficial in a dressing room littered with young players and certainly Celtic started to appear in the top five league positions, but the trophies still remained elusive.

100TH GOAL

It was a leap-year goal which proved to be Stevie Chalmers' 100th for the club as he netted a hat-trick against East Stirling on 29 February 1964. Despite success continuing to elude Celtic, Chalmers had still racked up an impressive tally of goals in that period, and duly passed the 100-mark at Celtic Park in front of a crowd of 15,000. It was the first goal of his hat-trick that day and it came inside the first minute of the match. He added another two in the course of the game, while fellow Century Bhoy, Bobby Murdoch also scored twice.

Season 1963/64 represented a personal triumph for Chalmers, who hit an impressive thirty-eight goals in all competitions, double the amount of Celtic's next best goalscorer, John Divers, and his tally included five in the European Cup-Winners' Cup. Celtic had reached the semi-final of the competition, and a 3–0 home win in the first leg of the semi-final against MTK Hungaria, when Chalmers scored two of the goals, gave the Hoops one foot in the final.

That was before a second-leg collapse in Hungary, when Celtic lost 4–0 on the night. Six of the players who would lift the European Cup three years later played that night – McNeill, Clark, Johnstone, Murdoch, Gemmell and Chalmers – and while there would have been obvious disappointment at the time over the manner of the defeat, it was an experience which would stand them in good stead in later European campaigns.

In just under five years, Stevie Chalmers had become only the fifteenth Celtic player at the time to score over 100 goals for the club, a mark of his quality and scoring prowess though he was less than halfway towards reaching his final tally of goals for the club.

LAST GOAL

The date, 1 May 1971 remains a poignant moment in Celtic's history because it was on this day that the Lisbon Lions appeared in a starting XI for the very last time. The team that ran out at Celtic Park, which was under reconstruction at the time, read: Simpson, Craig, Gemmell, Murdoch, McNeill, Clark, Johnstone, Wallace, Chalmers, Auld, Lennox.

They were the eleven men who had made history four years earlier when they lifted the European Cup in Lisbon and the 35,000 fans who gathered at Celtic Park that May day, for the final league game of the season against Clyde, remember that triumph as if it were yesterday.

Goalkeeper Ronnie Simpson, 'Faither' to his teammates because of his status as elder statesman of the team, had effectively retired due to injury, but still donned his kit and ran out with the 10 Hooped jerseys for the pre-match warm-up, but he was replaced by Evan Williams before the start of the game.

It was also the last game Bertie Auld played for the club, having been given a free transfer, and he was at his imperious best in midfield as Celtic ran out 6–1 winners

Bobby Lennox scored a hat-trick that day, while Willie Wallace scored twice. Clyde had the audacity to score a goal of their own but it was the man who had sealed the victory in Lisbon who netted the sixth and final goal of a special Celtic afternoon, firing home with twelve minutes of the match remaining.

It turned out to be Stevie Chalmers' last goal in his last competitive game for Celtic, and it was fitting that the man whose goal had effectively created the legend of the Lisbon Lions should score the last goal for that famous team.

In truth, the team from 1967 only played together a handful of times in the intervening four years, but they had ensured they would be forever remembered as the most famous starting XI in Celtic's history.

Chalmers left Celtic Park on 9 September 1971, joining Morton as player-coach, and he returned to Paradise nine days later as the blue and white Hoops of the Greenock side took on their more famous, and green, counterparts in a league match which the home side won 3–1. John Clark also played for Morton and scored an own goal.

HIGHS AND LOWS

Stevie Chalmers won four league championships between 1965 and 1969, though he also played a handful of games in the two title triumphs after that. He also won the Scottish Cup on three occasions, while he had four League Cup winner's medals and, of course, the European Cup.

It was in the 1969 League Cup final victory over St Johnstone that he suffered a broken leg, an injury that would effectively limit his playing time with Celtic after that.

A year earlier, he'd been part of Celtic's treble-winning side, playing in, though not scoring in the 6–2 League Cup final win over Hibernian when Bobby Lennox grabbed a hat-trick, and playing his part in the 4–0 demolition of Rangers in the Scottish Cup final.

Chalmers did score that day, rounding off the scoring with a brilliant solo goal with fifteen minutes of the match remaining, using his speed to get beyond the Rangers defence and firing in a shot at the near post to inflict the Ibrox side's first defeat in a Scottish Cup final for forty years.

Chalmers, a Celtic supporter to the core, liked scoring against Rangers, and he remains up to the end of season 2009/10, the last Celtic player to score a league hat-trick against the team's city rivals.

The goals came on 3 January 1966, as Celtic marched towards their first league title in twelve years, and it was a second-half demolition for the Hoops, who trailed 1–0 at half-time.

Chalmers netted the last of his, and Celtic's, goals in the final minute of the match and it was the clearest indication yet that the balance of power was shifting in Scottish football.

'Scoring a hat-trick is great for a striker but managing it against Rangers was a wee bit special and I'm amazed that it hasn't been repeated since then,' Chalmers said at the end of 2009. 'It's something that really stands out because it has been so long and I'm quite surprised that Henrik Larsson never managed it.'

And, of the goal that made hat-trick history, he said:

I don't even think I was thinking about a hat-trick after I scored my second goal. You're just thinking about scoring goals and not the actual number.

The last goal of the hat-trick came right in the final minute of the game and it was a very slack ball, I think the keeper shut his eyes when I got close to him and I just managed a wee poke over the top of him.

I recall that chipping it over the keeper made it the easiest of the three goals

I came into the dressing after the final whistle like a dog with four wagging tails because I was so up, but somewhere along the line, Big Jock said: 'I wouldn't give you Man of the Match, big Yogi was the top man today.'

That was typical of Big Jock. He was great at keeping your feet right down on the ground – but that record is still standing and there was Jock at the time playing the whole thing down.

AND ANOTHER THING ...

Like the rest of the Lisbon Lions, Stevie Chalmers was woefully underappreciated by his country, and only had five Scottish caps to his name. For a man who would score 231 goals for his club, including 13 in European competition, it was a scandalous total. But consider the other Lisbon Lions: Ronnie Simpson (5); Jim Craig (1); Tommy Gemmell (18); Bobby Murdoch (12); Billy McNeill (29); John Clark (4): Jimmy Johnstone (23); Willie Wallace (7): Stevie Chalmers (5); Bertie Auld (3); Bobby Lennox (10).

Their collective total is just 117, a figure that almost defies belief for a group of players who were among the very best in Europe during the late 1960s and early '70s. It's also safe to say that if they weren't plying their trade in the green and white Hoops of Celtic, then the number of Scotland gaps gained would have been considerably higher.

Stevie Chalmers' fourth and penultimate appearance in the dark blue of Scotland came against then reigning world Champions, Brazil on 25 June 1966 as the South Americans prepared to defend their crown in England.

The match at Hampden finished 1–1, and it was Chalmers who scored Scotland's goal in the first minute of the game – his third and final goal for his country – while his Celtic teammate John Clark performed an impressive marking job on Pele. And it was the Brazil No.10 jersey that Chalmers left with a souvenir of the match.

Reflecting on Stevie Chalmers' life and career, it should actually come as no surprise that he became a footballer. It seems to be in the Chalmers' genes. His son, Paul, followed in his footsteps, though he only made four appearances for Celtic, scoring one goal, while Stevie took after his father, David, who had played in the 1920s.

'He was a professional footballer and he, very quietly, was always there to help me,' Chalmers explained.

He taught me how to kick the ball and trap the ball and I always remember that he used to take me up to Springburn Park and would place the ball and try and hit the crossbar.

He was quite accurate at it and he encouraged me to practice and do the same. He played for Clydebank, back when they were more of a prominent senior team and he actually played alongside Jimmy McGrory. My Dad was a major influence on my career and I had always wanted to play football, I never really wanted to do anything else.

5

JIMMY QUINN

217 GOALS IN 331 GAMES

The small mining village of Croy in North Lanarkshire has always had a strong sense of community. The population has always been predominately Irish and Catholic. It should come as no surprise to learn that, like other villages of its kind across Scotland, Celtic Football Club is a way of life for almost everyone.

Where Croy differs from most other towns and villages is that it has its very own Celtic legend. For the children who populate the streets of Croy, proudly showing off their replica kits, Jimmy Quinn is a mystical character, the stuff of legend from the distant past. Yet, this Celtic superhero did exist and he served his club and community with distinction. David Potter's excellent book, *The Mighty Quinn*, labels him Celtic's first goalscoring hero. That is a fitting summation of a man who left an indelible mark on the club that he loved. Quinn, quite simply, was a phenomenon.

A coal miner by trade and the son of Irish immigrants, Quinn was plucked from Croy club, Smithston Albion, by Willie Maley and catapulted into the Celtic first team. His strength and bravery are well-documented by now, but Quinn wasn't the hulking centre forward people think. Standing at less than 5 ft 9in, he started off on the left wing before drifting into the centre, where his real quality shone. While height wasn't his biggest asset, he more than made up for this with skill, attitude and application. He took some rough treatment, but he could dish it out too.

Strangely, for someone so assured on the pitch, Quinn was apparently the epitome of shyness off the pitch. It is said that he preferred the quiet life and that is given as the reason for him turning down Sunderland's approach before signing for Celtic. Even then, Maley had to work hard to secure his services and was initially knocked back on more than one occasion. However, the perseverance was more than worth it. Quinn, after being moved to centre forward by Maley, showcased his prodigious scoring talent. He played 331 times for Celtic and scored 217 goals – a staggering strike-rate in any era of the game. His record of twenty hat-tricks is bettered only by Jimmy McGrory. He was also the shining light of the first hugely successful Celtic side, a team that dominated Scottish football and played the Celtic Way.

Trophies came at an impressive rate during Quinn's time at Celtic. He won six league titles and five Scottish Cups. When Celtic ruled the roost in Scotland with six consecutive league titles between 1904 and 1910, Quinn was the talisman; the striker who always delivered for his team. In terms of titles, this was then a record achievement for Celtic and Quinn led from the front. He was irresistible. Teammates adored him, supporters idolised him and opposition defences simply could not handle him. He was the perfect centre forward in every respect.

Quinn played for Celtic between 1900 and 1915, but his legend lives on – in Croy and beyond. The absence of video footage means that generations of Celtic supporters haven't been able to gain a complete understanding of his talents, but the written tributes are flattering. Most also carry the quote from Maley that summed up the impact Quinn, that shy miner from Croy, had on Celtic. 'He was the keystone in the greatest team Celtic ever had.'

FIRST GOAL

Willie Maley was perplexed as he took a deep breath and once again asked Jimmy Quinn to sign for Celtic. The club's manager didn't always get his way but he had never expected to have any bother in convincing Quinn that he should sign for Celtic. He had the talent to be a Celtic player and came from a background that ensured he had a soft spot for the club. He was from Croy, a Celtic stronghold where everyone wanted to play for Celtic. This was Quinn's big chance. Maley had offered him the golden ticket. But he wasn't budging.

Why was Quinn reluctant? Firstly, he had reservations about his own ability. He was a star for Smithston Albion in the Juniors but he didn't feel good enough to play professionally for Celtic. He never had the faith in his talent that Maley evidently did. Quinn did not believe he could go to Celtic and make a telling contribution. Secondly, he didn't want to move to Glasgow. He wanted to stay in Croy. Eventually, Maley smoothed the waters, told Quinn he could commute the fifteen miles from Croy to Glasgow and got his target to sign a provisional form on 30 December 1900.

Quinn played in an Inter-City League match against Third Lanark on 31 December and didn't score in a 1–1 draw, but he'd caught the bug. Maley was at his charming best as he entertained the Quinn family and, pointedly, invited Jimmy to training and games. By 12 January 1901, he was ready to pop the question again and this time Quinn had no hesitation. He was a Celtic player and delighted with the news. That day saw the birth of a legend. Quinn and Celtic was a match made in heaven.

Every glorious story starts with a small step. Quinn made his competitive debut against St Mirren on 19 January and scored in a 4–3 win. He was shattered by half-time, physically drained, but his first goal was a huge boost for him and Maley was impressed. The manager had worked hard to sign Quinn and, while the new recruit was still short of full fitness, he was showing a lot of promise.

It was an exciting time for Quinn although Celtic's only hope of glory was in the Scottish Cup. Quinn spent a great deal of time playing for the reserves but forced his way into the first team before too long and was named in the starting line-up for the 1901 Scottish Cup final against Hearts. Quinn scored that day, a virtuoso solo goal that saw him slalom past six defenders, but Celtic lost the game 4–3 to the Edinburgh side. His hope of a first medal had been dashed. Thankfully, it wasn't a sign of things to come.

100TH GOAL

Between the years of 1904 and 1910, Celtic were unstoppable. Between 1904 and 1910, Jimmy Quinn was unstoppable. It should come as no surprise then, to learn that Quinn completed his century of Celtic goals during that period of complete dominance when Willie Maley's side won six consecutive championships from 1904/05 to 1909/10. In every single one of those seasons, Quinn finished as Celtic's top scorer. Not only that, from 1903/04 until 1912/13 Quinn finished as Celtic's top marksman. He was playing at the peak of his powers.

Oddly, though, his 100th goal came in a rare defeat for Celtic in season 1907/08. Celtic travelled north to play Aberdeen in the league and Quinn's goal could not stop a 2–1 defeat. It was a rare blip in another season of dominance for Celtic. In fact, Quinn and Co lost just three games that season as they won the league with a haul of 55 points. Falkirk finished runners-up, while Quinn scored once as St Mirren were beaten 5–1 in the Scottish Cup final.

Quinn finished that season with nineteen of Celtic's eighty-six league goals. His best tally for a league campaign came in 1906/07, when he scored twenty-nine goals. That haul also saw him crowned Scotland's top scorer. During the six-in-a-row period, Quinn helped Celtic win the Scottish Cup twice. Overall, he finished with five Scottish Cup winner's medals from his time at Celtic. Those 100 goals became 200 in the years that followed. If it hadn't been for injury that haunted him in the last years of his Celtic career, Quinn's tally would have been even higher. Naturally, Celtic's trophy count would have been increased too.

LAST GOAL

In an ideal world, Jimmy Quinn would have bowed out of Celtic on a real high. His Celtic story merited one last moment in the sun, a winning goal in the Scottish Cup final to round everything off. Football is rarely as romantic as that. Instead, Quinn's last goal for Celtic came against Hamilton Accies on Boxing Day 1914. It was a typical Quinn finish. Low, hard and out of the goalkeeper's reach. Just the way he liked them.

There were no frills but Quinn never tended to mess about. In truth, it was nothing short of a miracle that Quinn was playing at all. Injury meant that he had only played two games in season 1913/14 and he practically semi-retired the next season. By then, he was seen as a trusted assistant to Maley and played only in emergencies. Yet, he could still make an impact, with that goal against Hamilton – the winner naturally – illustrating his golden touch.

By the end of the season, having played just six games, Quinn knew that his Celtic career was drawing to a close. His final outing had come against Hearts at the end of January 1915. He played through the pain barrier that day as he brought his Celtic career to an end. He had given everything to the club and left with the respect of everyone associated with Celtic. What did he do next? Quinn, although he had come out of his shell a little, opted for the simple life and worked as a miner. Yet, he still followed Celtic and was a regular visitor to the stadium in the years that followed. When once he had been a shining light for the Croy Bhoys on the pitch, he now stood alongside his village friends on the terraces. Celtic went deep into the heart of Quinn.

Jimmy died on 21 November 1945 after a short illness. He had remained in Croy all of his days with his beloved family and continued to work as a miner. There were never any airs or graces about him. He never wanted any preferential treatment. Visit Croy now and you will see a tribute to him in the social club in the village. Many of his family members reside in the village and its surrounds. It is well over 100 years since Quinn first kicked a ball for Celtic, but his spirit lives on.

HIGHS AND LOWS

The myriad of trophies won by Jimmy Quinn and glut of goals he scored are obvious highlights. Yet, the most famous game from his glorious Celtic career came against Rangers in the 1904 Scottish Cup final on 16 April. Trailing 2–0 after just twelve minutes, Celtic needed inspiration and Quinn provided it. He scored a hat-trick to complete a remarkable comeback and wrote his name into the history books at the same time. It was a stunning achievement in what became known as 'The Quinn Final'.

The first goal was a solo effort of incredible skill and power. Just before half-time, he converted a cross from Bobby Orr to make it 2–2. Rangers couldn't handle him and the winner arrived ten minutes before the end. Again, Quinn's finishing was adroit as the Celtic players and supporters celebrated. For Quinn, it was routine. There was no grandstanding when the hat-trick was complete. It was all part of his job. Within the crowd of 64,323 at Hampden that day, many of Quinn's friends and family from Croy went wild with celebration. Yet, they were worshipping a reluctant hero.

If that was his Scottish Cup highlight for Celtic, he didn't have to wait too long for a low point. It came in the following season's competition when Celtic met Rangers in the semi-final and Quinn was found guilty of violent conduct against Rangers defender Alec Craig. Quinn, in actual fact, was guilty of nothing but the referee, Tom Robertson, didn't see it that way. Ignoring the pleas of Craig, who defended Quinn, he sent the Celtic striker off. Quinn was eventually banned for a month. Again, Craig appealed on his behalf. Again, those pleas were ignored. It was an early controversy in Scottish football. It wouldn't be the last.

Indeed, Quinn, while a quiet character off the pitch, had to deal with a few controversies on it; few compared to the mess of 1907 when he was banned for two months after again being found guilty of violent conduct after a clash with Rangers defender Joe Hendry. It was alleged that Quinn kicked him in the face. This, remember, was in the days before blanket media coverage but it was still a massive news story across Scotland. Quinn defended himself, saying that the collision was accidental, but documentation on the incident seems to suggest the SFA were eager to make an example of him. Other observers state that, given the severity of the allegation, he was lucky not to be banned *sine die*.

Whatever the truth, and people still argue about it, the Celtic family rallied around Quinn. Money was raised by supporters to cover his wages and Quinn was the guest of honour at a concert in Glasgow, from which the proceeds went to charity. All he could say was 'thanks.' He was a humble man and this sort of adulation was simply too much for him. Yet, it summed up what Quinn had become at Celtic. He was one of the first heroes.

AND ANOTHER THING ...

It seems Jimmy Quinn had a monopoly on nicknames. 'The Mighty Quinn' is probably the most famous, while he was also regularly referred to as 'The Equator' (The Centre of the Earth). This alluded to his central role in his all-conquering Celtic team of the early twentieth century. Another nickname was 'Jamie the Silent', as a result of his calm, quiet exterior. That was later temporarily changed to 'Jamie the Sullen' after his different brushes with the football authorities.

Legend tells us that Quinn's brother, Peter, played as a guest for Celtic on a couple of occasions. Quinn's grandson, also Jimmy, played for Celtic between 1963 and 1974, making a total of forty-one appearances and scoring one goal. He had a hard act to follow, but was an honest, talented player who just happened to be competing for a place in officially the strongest Celtic side of all time. He sadly passed away at a relatively young age.

On the international scene, Quinn represented Scotland eleven times and scored seven goals between 1905 and 1912. Of Irish origin, his Scotland selection was viewed as a major breakthrough for the community. Ironically, he made his debut against Ireland. He scored in a 2–0 win over England in 1910 and grabbed four goals in a 5–0 rout of Northern Ireland in 1908.

6

PATSY GALLACHER

192 GOALS IN 464 GAMES

Looks can be deceiving. When Patsy Gallacher walked in to Celtic Park for the first time in 1911, he was a mere slip of a boy. Celtic icon Jimmy Quinn, a brute compared to this frail young Irishman, had genuine concern over how the eighteen-year-old would cope when he was put in against the hard men of the Scottish senior league. 'If you put that wee thing out on the park you'll get done for manslaughter,' is what the Mighty Quinn is supposed to have said to Willie Maley, but the Celtic manager was unperturbed. He had seen Gallacher play for Clydebank Juniors and felt he was good enough for Celtic. His judgement would be vindicated in some style.

The absence of video footage makes it impossible to ascertain just how good Gallacher was but, despite his lack of height, history tells us that he was head and shoulders above everyone else during his days as a Celt. He played for Celtic between 1911 and 1926 and lit up the Scottish game. Gallacher, nicknamed the 'Mighty Atom' was a bundle of skill, bravery and energy. In his prime, he was undoubtedly one of the best players in the world.

Patsy played for Celtic for fifteen years and etched his name into club folklore in golden letters. He was the best show in town and fans gathered at Celtic Park to see this born entertainer in action. He was skilful, composed and a fierce competitor. There was no such thing as a lost cause for Patsy and he also knew his way towards goal. He played most of his career at Celtic as an inside-right and was expected to fill the playmaker role. Gallacher did that wonderfully well but also managed to score 192 goals in 464 games, which is a staggering return.

In terms of silverware, Gallacher also got the rewards. He won six league championships with Celtic and four Scottish Cups. The national tournament would give him his first Celtic medal in 1912 and also his last in 1925. That game has become known as the 'Patsy Gallacher Final' due to the incredible, ingenious goal he scored against Dundee in Celtic's triumph. It's a fitting way to remember a true Celtic legend.

FIRST GOAL

Born in Milford, County Donegal, in 1892, Patrick Gallacher moved to Scotland with his family and settled in Clydebank. He started work as an apprentice shipbuilder and combined his day job with a fledgling career in football. As a teenager, there was hardly a pick on him but he showed himself to be made of strong stuff as he forged a huge reputation in the Junior game with Clydebank.

Several Scottish sides showed an interest, but he agreed to play a few trial matches for Celtic and won everybody over in spectacular fashion. Any doubts as to whether his fragile frame could stand up to the demands of the senior game were dispersed when, as a trialist, he scored twice in a 6–1 win over Dumfries and grabbed a hat-trick in a 5–0 victory over the British Army. Those games might have been treated as friendlies, but Celtic had unearthed a gem and signed Patsy on 25 October 1911.

Gallacher made his Celtic debut on 2 December 1911, in a game against St Mirren as goals from Andy Donaldson, Peter

Johnstone and Willie Loney gave the 12,000 crowd and young Patsy a day to remember. He was off and running and his first goal wouldn't be long in arriving. Queen's Park were next up for Celtic and he was on target as his new club won 4–1 at Hampden. It was the first goal but wouldn't be the last that Gallacher would score at the national stadium.

Celtic finished second in the league that season but there was joy to be found in the Scottish Cup. He had played only one Scottish Cup game prior to that 1912 final, the semi-final 3–0 win over Hearts, but Willie Maley showed faith in the teenager and handed him a start against Clyde at Hampden. The young Patsy stood alongside the two Jimmys, Quinn and McMenemy, as Celtic fought for the silverware and managed to score in a 2–0 win at Hampden. Just five months into his Celtic career, he was teaming up with the greats and scoring in finals. It couldn't get any better than this. But it did.

100TH GOAL

Patsy Gallacher started season 1916/17 by scoring four goals as Celtic beat St Mirren 5–1 in the first league game of the campaign. On the last day of the season, he scored again as Celtic routed Clyde 5–0. By then, Celtic had claimed their fourth successive league title and Gallacher was in his pomp. He was inspirational for that dominant Celtic side. Helped by the likes of Jimmy McColl, Andy McAtee and Jimmy McMenemy, Gallacher was an icon of the Celtic support.

He also became a Century Bhoy that season. McColl would finish as Celtic's top scorer with twenty-four goals that year, but Gallacher was a regular name on the scoresheet for Celtic and his 100th strike for the club came on 14 April 1917, in a 1–0 away win against Hibernian. Celtic had already secured the championship by that stage, but it was an impressive milestone for Gallacher to reach just six years into his Celtic career.

Up until the start of the four-in-a-row run in 1913/14, Patsy had to content himself with a solitary Scottish Cup medal from his Celtic career. Yet, that all changed when Celtic won the double. With the great Jimmy Quinn edging towards the end of his illustrious career, it was a time for new heroes and Gallacher led from the front as his goals and unique creativity helped spearhead Celtic's double challenge. The league was won by six points from Rangers and so began a period of dominance that would last for four years. Gallacher would score the bulk of his first 100 goals during that period as he put Celtic back where the club belongs – at the top of Scottish football.

LAST GOAL

It was a moment that could have graced the finest Hollywood sports film. The year was 1925. The event was the Scottish Cup final and the star attraction was Patsy Gallacher. The Irishman remained the darling of the Celtic support and there he was at Hampden – fourteen years after making his Celtic debut – trying to steer his beloved club to more silverware. He was now approaching his mid-thirties but Patsy wanted to show he could still do it on the biggest stage. He delivered with one of the best goals the game has ever seen.

On 11 April 1925, Dundee were Celtic's opponents. The Celtic team that day was Shevlin, W. McStay, Hilley, Wilson, J. McStay, McFarlane, Connolly, Gallacher, McGrory, Thomson and McLean, and Willie Maley's men were trailing 1–0 with just twenty minutes remaining. Enter Gallacher with one of the most wondrous goals in the history of football to haul Celtic level, and give Jimmy McGrory the platform to score a late winner.

What made Gallacher's goal so special? Everything. He is said to have lost his balance three times as he embarked on a mazy run into the box that left the Dundee defenders bewildered. With every jink, twist and turn, he edged closer to the goal and eventually found himself one-on-one with the Dundee goalkeeper Jock Britton. With the ball clasped between his feet, Patsy's genius was summed up when he somersaulted over the goalkeeper and landed in the net with the ball still in his possession. He had equalised in the most spectacular fashion and received a standing ovation from the 75,000 fans inside Hampden.

Gallacher would stay with Celtic for another season but appearances would be few and far between due to injury. Indeed, that remarkable Scottish Cup final goal would prove to be his last strike in Celtic colours. The club, in another of its questionable historic decisions, decided that Patsy was done and retired him in July 1926, without the player's knowledge. Naturally, Gallacher was fuming. 'I'm as right as rain,' was his response and he went on to show that his knee injury wasn't as bad as Celtic thought by playing on for six years for Falkirk.

Patsy played until 1932 before retiring as he neared the age of forty. He spent his latter days running the International Bar in Clydebank and also brought up six children after his wife died tragically in childbirth. Patsy looked on proudly as two of his boys, Willie and Tommy, entered the professional ranks. They never hit the heights of their father but few players did. Patsy Gallacher wasn't just a Celtic great, he was a football great.

HIGHS AND LOWS

Patsy Gallacher enjoyed a glittering career with Celtic and the highs are plentiful. His first and last medals for the club came in the Scottish Cup and he scored in both finals, 1912 and 1925.

The latter, which kick-started Celtic's comeback in a 2–1 win over Dundee, will go down in history as one of the best cup final goals of all time, anywhere in the world. Over the course of his fifteen-year Celtic career, he added another two Scottish Cup triumphs – in 1914 and 1923 – to bring his overall tally to four.

The league was also relatively kind to Gallacher, who won a total of six championships with Celtic. He was an integral part of the four-in-a-row run between 1914 and 1917, and was a virtual ever-present in seasons 1918/19 and 1921/22, as Celtic were again crowned champions of Scotland. The 1921/22 triumph, coming ten years after he had signed for Celtic, must have been especially sweet for Gallacher. It also turned out to be the last league title he won during his Celtic career.

During those years, there were a multitude of vital goals but the precocious Gallacher also had a knack for the spectacular. He was there to entertain and his style of play often led to him scoring the type of goals that other, less gifted, players could only dream about. The best was obviously his wonder strike against Dundee in the Scottish Cup final, but he also left the entire Hibernian team in his wake as he jinked past eleven challenges on his way to scoring a staggering solo goal in a 2–1 defeat in 1921. That was what Gallacher was capable of and throughout his career, even Rangers greats would regularly pay tribute to his skill.

It wasn't all highs though. He would have liked to have had more success in the Scottish Cup, even though the tournament was suspended between 1915 and 1919, while Celtic's failure to win the league championship in 1917/18 frustrated Gallacher, especially as they clinched the title the following season and could have been celebrating six-in-a-row. Given the success of Jimmy Quinn and Co. in the previous decade, that feat would have meant the world to Patsy.

The nadir of his Celtic career, however, undoubtedly came in 1926 when the club's custodians decided to call time on his days at Celtic. They cited a knee injury but Patsy knew he wasn't finished. Falkirk eventually paid £1,500 for his services and he gave them six sterling years before retiring in 1932. It was a mistake on the club's part and they would find success hard to come by after Gallacher's departure. Who knows what would have happened had he stayed?

AND ANOTHER THING ...

Patsy Gallacher started off a real family dynasty in football. The Celtic legend's children, Tommy and Willie, both played the game professionally and Willie's son Kevin had great success in the modern game with spells at Dundee United, Coventry City and Blackburn Rovers. In 1988, Kevin – some sixty-three years after his grandfather had famously won the Scottish Cup for Celtic – scored against the Hoops at Hampden in the 1988 final. He fired his Dundee United side ahead with a ferocious volley, but Celtic hit back with two late goals from Frank McAvennie.

Confusion surrounds both Patsy's surname and height, with varying spellings and numbers being given in the history books. Some people spell his surname 'Gallagher', but the most common version is 'Gallacher'. The Irish spelling is Ó Gallchobhair and legend tells us that it was originally given as 'Gallagher' when the family first arrived in Scotland. However, through time, that was changed to 'Gallacher', with one rumoured reason for this being that this was the spelling on their front door nameplate. In terms of height, he is recorded as being anything from 5ft 5in to 5ft 9in.

During his Celtic career, Patsy finished as the club's top scorer on three separate occasions. In 1912/13, he shared the honour with Jimmy Quinn (11 goals) and the following season he scored 24 times to top the charts. In 1917/18, he also finished ahead of his teammates with 17 goals. During his fifteen years as a Celt, he also scored nine hat-tricks.

In the international arena, Gallacher played eleven times for Northern Ireland and also represented the Irish Free State. In addition, he was capped by the Scottish League Select on two occasions. His grandson, Kevin, went on to play for Scotland and appeared at the 1998 World Cup.

7

JOHN HUGHES

189 GOALS IN 416 APPEARANCES

Celtic scouts always used to monitor the junior ranks for up and coming talent and their attention was drawn towards Shotts' Hannah Park in the late days of the 1950s. The subject of their interest was a young forward by the name of John Hughes. A hulking presence, with real size, speed and strength, Hughes later earned the nickname 'Yogi' in reference to the cartoon bear. The boy could play, of that there was no doubt, and Celtic made him an offer. On 3 October 1959, Hughes became a Celtic player.

He was only seventeen at the time and added a youthful exuberance to the Celtic squad when he made his debut the next year. At times, he was unpredictable and it's fair to say he could excite and frustrate supporters in equal measure as a player. Hughes had class though and it shone at Celtic. At 6ft 2in, he was a big man who carried his frame well, but he had great close control and the ability to breeze past people by using all of his attributes. He also had a penchant for the spectacular when it came to scoring goals.

Until the arrival of Jock Stein, the first half of the 1960s were mostly forgettable for Celtic, but Hughes was one of the club's most effective players during a difficult period. His goals could not aid a successful title challenge from Celtic but he helped the club reach three finals in the pre-Stein era. On each occasion, Celtic failed. It was clear the club was underachieving in a considerable way but the arrival of Stein, in 1965, changed all that. He created the best team in Celtic's history.

Under the new manager, Celtic swept all before them and Hughes played a major part in the success. He officially won eleven major honours but deserved a European Cup winner's medal as much as the rest of his teammates. He never played in that 1967 final, but started five games on the road to Lisbon and is regarded as a Lion like the rest. In 1970, Hughes did play as Celtic faced Feyenoord in the club's second European Cup final but a 2–1 loss left Yogi devastated.

Hughes left Celtic for Crystal Palace in 1971, but is remembered as a committed, talented and effective forward from a period when the club had an embarrassment of riches in that department. When he was on his game and scoring goals, leaving defenders bewildered and using all his attributes to full effect, there were few better than Hughes. The fact that he never played in Lisbon should not affect the perception of his contribution for Celtic, before and during the Stein era. Hughes' goals and trophies demonstrate his value. He is a Celtic great.

'I don't think that there is another group of players in Celtic's history that get that special attention we do,' he says of the Stein team.

It perhaps helps that most of us were Scots and were born and brought up so close to the stadium. With the finances and the way the game has gone today, it would take an absolute miracle for that to happen again. We loved the club and had a special rapport with the supporters, mainly because we were supporters ourselves.

FIRST GOAL

To paraphrase a popular football cliché, the 1960s was a decade of two halves. Between 1960 and 24 April 1965, when Celtic won the Scottish Cup, there was precious little to get excited about. However, John Hughes went about his business in the most professional of manners as he embarked on a long and successful Celtic career by doing what he did best – scoring goals. The versatile attacker averaged around twenty goals per season in the first half of the decade, despite Celtic's lack of silverware.

Hughes' first goal came on his debut against Third Lanark on 13 August 1960. Celtic won 2–0 and Hughes scored once. He impressed and recovered from an early miss to break his Celtic duck. In a personal sense, Hughes never looked back as he marked his first League Cup campaign with a total of five goals. Celtic, however, would be knocked out at the group stages.

Celtic finished fourth in the league that season, but at least they made progress to the final of the Scottish Cup in 1961. Hughes played in both games as Celtic dominated, but drew 0–0 with Dunfermline in the final, and then lost the replay 2–0. It was an early cup disappointment in Hughes' Celtic career and he would have to get used to that sort of blow for the next four years.

Prior to Jock Stein's arrival in 1965, Hughes never played in a Celtic side that finished higher than third in the league. Other than the 1961 Scottish Cup final, Hughes' Celtic only played in two other showpiece matches before 1965 – the final of the 1963 Scottish Cup and 1964 League Cup. On both occasions, Celtic played Rangers and they lost twice. The 1963 match went to a replay after a 1–1 draw and Rangers won 3–0. In 1964, the Ibrox side won 2–1. Hughes played in all of those matches.

Yet, despite not getting his hands on any silverware, Hughes had shown himself to be a real asset to Celtic. His versatility helped him, as did his knack for scoring goals. Yogi was always a big man and he used his size to his advantage and was deadly when given a chance. He was scoring the goals but Celtic weren't getting the silverware to make his contribution worthy. Hughes couldn't have done much more but he would soon get his rewards.

100TH GOAL

Jock Stein won twenty-five major trophies as Celtic manager, but John Hughes' 100th goal takes us back to when those glory days started in the triumphant 1965 Scottish Cup campaign. In fact, the match that marked Hughes' century of goals – against Kilmarnock in a 3–2 quarter-final win – took place just three days before Stein's return to Celtic as manager. Hughes was joined on the scoresheet by Bobby Lennox and Bertie Auld that day.

Celtic, who had been beaten 2–1 by Rangers in the League Cup final and went on to finish a lowly eighth in the league, desperately needed to end the season on a high and the Scottish Cup would provide the respite and confidence boost that Stein's new men craved. Hughes, who finished as Celtic's top league scorer with twenty-two goals, was retained in the team by the new manager as they homed in on silverware.

After a 2–2 semi-final draw with Motherwell, Celtic beat the Fir Park side 3–0 in a replay. Hughes was on fire that season and scored that day, as did Bobby Lennox and Stevie Chalmers. Celtic, with Stein at the helm, had reached the cup final and had the perfect chance to finish the season in perfect fashion. More than that, it was the chance to win the first major honour since 1957.

In truth, it was an opportunity to inject some much-needed pride back into the club. All that stood in Celtic's way was Dunfermline Athletic.

In the modern era, Celtic have met Dunfermline in Scottish Cup finals in 2004 and 2007. On both occasions, Celtic were over-whelming favourites for the match. Yet, back on 24 April 1965, things were slightly different. Celtic finished eighth in the league, while the Pars were only a point behind eventual winners Kilmarnock. This was by no means a straightforward task for Celtic. In fact, they were probably expected to lose the game and Dunfermline proved a tough nut to crack.

Twice, Celtic were behind in the game. Hughes lined up at centre forward and looked on as Dunfermline took the lead. Auld equalised but the Fife side took the lead again, only for the Bhoy Bertie to strike early in the second half and leave the scores at 2–2. The game was finally balanced and then, in eighty-one minutes, came a pivotal moment in Celtic's history. Charlie Gallagher floated a perfect corner into the box and Billy McNeill powered home a header. Celtic were ahead for the first time in the game and the cup was on its way to Paradise. Stein was off and running.

LAST GOAL

Between John Hughes' first and 100th goals for Celtic, he won no major honours for the club. Between his 100th goal and final strike, his 189th, he won six league titles, one Scottish Cup and four League Cups. Celtic were in the midst of a golden era and Hughes was right in the thick of it. From the years of 1965 to 1971, when the forward left the club, Stein's Celtic were unstop-pable and Hughes played more often than not.

It all came to an end on 19 October 1971, as Celtic accepted a bid from Crystal Palace and Hughes, against his wishes, was let go by Stein. It's fair to say that Hughes' relationship with the Celtic manager was never the same after that. Yogi's last game for Celtic was against Copenhagen in a European Cup tie. His last goal came against Ayr United in a 3–0 away win in the League Cup on 21 August 1971.

Off Yogi went to London and Crystal Palace. He displayed his talents with a spectacular strike that featured on the Match of the Day credits for a while. It came against Sheffield United and was voted second in the English Goal of the Season Awards. He ended up staying at Palace for around sixteen months before moving to Sunderland. His spell at Roker Park was short-lived. Yogi played fifteen minutes of football before succumbing to an injury that would force him to retire. The career of a Celtic great came to an unfortunate end.

HIGHS AND LOWS

John Hughes' Celtic career can be divided into two distinct parts: his domestic and European experiences. On reflection, he encountered highs and lows in both environments, but it's probably best to start with life in the Scottish game because without domestic success there would have been no European football. Not that success always came easily for Hughes in the Scottish game.

As stated earlier, the early 1960s were a hellish time for Celtic as a club. Hughes, personally, was a success story but Celtic's league form was patchy at best, while trophies proved elusive. Even when Celtic did reach cup finals, they always lost. Hughes, a young man learning his trade, was doing all the right things but he just couldn't help Celtic to silverware, no matter how hard he tried.

Jock Stein's arrival signalled the end of the domestic lows. Instead, Celtic embarked on the highest of highs and Hughes won the first of his six league titles in 1965/66. He would go on to win a league winner's medal every year for the remainder of his Celtic career. It just became the norm for the Celtic players of that era and Hughes played a major role in each of the championship wins.

In cup competition, he won the Scottish Cup in 1965 but wouldn't play in another victorious final. He was on the losing side against Rangers in 1966, missed out in 1967, was injured in 1969, was on the losing side in 1970 and left out the following year as Celtic beat Rangers 2–1 in a final. Unbelievably, Yogi would walk away from Celtic Park with just one Scottish Cup medal.

In the League Cup, he was more successful. In 1965, Hughes coolly converted two pressurised penalties to give Celtic a 2–1 win over Rangers at Hampden. It would be the first of five successive triumphs in the tournament and Hughes would pick up winner's medals in 1966, 1967 and 1969. He was injured in 1968 and missed out in 1970.

Then there was Europe. Hughes, having picked up an injury in the weeks before the 1967 final, never regained his place for the Lisbon tie. The fact that others like Charlie Gallagher and the prolific Joe McBride, who was cruelly injured, also missed out was of little consolation to Hughes. Nothing would soften the blow of missing those games, although Hughes did get to grace a European Cup final in 1970 when Celtic, strong favourites, lost to Dutch side Feyenoord. Which of these disappointments affected Hughes the most? It is simply impossible to say. Celtic, of course, went on to compete in the Intercontinental Club Championship against Racing Club. Hughes played in the game at Hampden and then in the play-off as Celtic lost out in the controversial tie.

Another European low point came against MTK Hungaria in the semi-final of the Cup-Winners' Cup in 1964. Hughes had been excellent on that cup run. He scored a hat-trick against Basel in the first round and also netted a crucial, and sublime, away goal against Slovan Bratislava. Celtic then faced the Hungarians in the last four and a 3–0 first leg win at Celtic Park set them up perfectly. However, they went to Budapest and attacked instead of protecting their lead and lost 4–0.

'Looking back, we were unbelievably naïve,' said Hughes, who had a goal chalked off. 'Bob Kelly was the man in charge and he said, "We've beaten them at home and now we'll beat them over there." It was dreadfully complacent.'

Yet, while Hughes had his fair share of lows in Europe, it would be remiss to leave out arguably his greatest display in a Celtic strip, which came against Leeds United in the second leg of the European Cup semi-final. Up against Jack Charlton, Hughes was immense and scored Celtic's first as Stein's men won 2–1 to seal a 3–1 aggregate victory over the much-fancied English side. Yogi ranks it as his favourite ever game for Celtic. 'It was one of my favourite goals and I am glad I scored on such a fantastic night, the feeling was incredible,' said Yogi. 'I think it was the most important goal I ever scored for the club.'

AND ANOTHER THING ...

If the going was soft or heavy, John Hughes was a happy man. Let the game begin. If the going was hard, the Celtic striker knew there could be trouble ahead. Every footballer has their idiosyncrasies. Some don't like the wind, others hate the rain. Hughes simply hated playing on rock-solid pitches. Given the Scottish climate, you can imagine that this caused a bit of a problem for the Celtic striker and that was the case, until he found an ingenious solution on Boxing Day 1964.

Instead of trying to get by wearing studs or moulded boots, Hughes never wore any boots. Instead, he spotted Billy McNeill's rubber-soled sandshoes and asked if he could try them out in a game against Motherwell. Cesar agreed to the request and Yogi found the answer to his problems. This was his Eureka moment. He scored twice in that particular game and then famously grabbed five goals while wearing them in an 8–0 win over Aberdeen on 30 January 1965.

Yogi's 189 goals came during twelve years at Celtic Park and twice he finished as the club's top scorer. He scored 26 goals in season 1961/62 and followed that up with a 21-goal haul in the following campaign. He scored an impressive nine hat-tricks for Celtic, seven of which came in the league, one in the League Cup and one in Europe, against Basel in September 1963.

In total, Yogi made eight appearances for the Scotland national side and scored one goal, which came against England in a 1–1 draw at Hampden in February 1968. 134,000 fans watched that game and Yogi was joined in the Scotland team by Celtic team-mates Ronnie Simpson, Tommy Gemmell, Billy McNeill and Bobby Lennox.

Hughes' brother, Billy, was also a professional footballer and is regarded as a legend at Sunderland, where he made over 300 appearances and helped the club win the FA Cup in 1973. A talented winger, Billy played for Scotland. Yogi also had a spell at Sunderland in 1973, but was injured within fifteen minutes of his debut and never played for the club again. The injury forced him to retire from playing in October 1973.

Yogi's career came full circle when he returned to where it all started for him at Shotts to become the manager of the successful junior side. He also coached Baillieston Juniors but never had a foray into the senior side of the coaching game, although he did manage the Scotland junior side for a four-year spell between 1978 and 1982.

8

SANDY McMAHON

177 GOALS IN 217 APPEARANCES

In the pantheon of Celtic greats, the name of Alexander McMahon must rank alongside some of the more illustrious or well-known names that immediately spring to mind. Indeed, it could be argued that McMahon, better known as 'Sandy', and often eulogised by supporters of the time as 'the Duke', was the very first legend of the club. Certainly, he was the first player to pass the 100-goal mark and for that alone he deserves to be recognised.

He also stands at the head of a great goalscoring lineage which has stretched down through the 122 years of Celtic's history. After McMahon came Jimmy Quinn, then Patsy Gallacher and Jimmy McGrory in the pre-Second World War era, to be followed later by the likes of Bobby Lennox, Stevie Chalmers, Kenny Dalglish and Henrik Larsson.

There were others, many of who will be lionised on these pages, but McMahon came first and set the standards for others to follow. That his Celtic career spanned the late nineteenth and early twentieth centuries is one factor why his name and exploits are not as widely known or celebrated as they should be, but the history books have recorded the 177 goals he scored for Celtic in 217 appearances and that marks him out as a special talent, as well as being the eighth top goalscorer in the club's history.

In his book, *The Story of the Celtic,* Willie Maley said of McMahon that he:

… was one of the club's earliest stars and certainly one of its brightest, and was regarded as the most marvellous header of the ball of the period.

Tall, almost ungainly in appearance, Sandy depended on footwork and the deceptive swerve to beat an opponent. Of speed he had little. His judgement of the flight of the ball when free or corner kicks were being taken was simply marvellous, and despite the fact that there were always several opponents set to watch him, at these times he scored a great number of goals with his head.

Although he was regarded as a centre forward during the very short time he spent with Hibernians *(sic)* before coming to Parkhead, it was as an inside left he made his reputation in partnership with Johnny Campbell, who in those days played on the wing.

McMahon was an integral part of Celtic's first trophy successes, with the Scottish Cup win of 1892 followed a year later by the club's very first league championship. He was a goalscorer, but also a dribbler in the finest Celtic tradition. It was he, along with the likes of Campbell and Johnny Madden, who provided entertainment and artistry to football and the Celtic team in particular, beginning a tradition of playing football that has evolved down through the years and has become known as 'the Celtic way'.

Sandy McMahon was still a relatively young man when he passed away in 1916 – he was only forty-five years old – but he had ensured a lasting place in the annals of Celtic history. He was, and remains, a true Celtic Great. He won't be the last but he was probably the first.

FIRST GOAL

Having joined Celtic from Hibernian just five days before Christmas 1890, it would be over a month before Sandy McMahon pulled on the green and white stripes in earnest. His debut came in a 3–1 league defeat away to Vale of Leven on 24 January 1891, though he would enjoy better fortunes against the same opposition later in the season.

It was the inaugural season for the Scottish League, with ten teams competing to be the very first champions of Scotland – Celtic, Dumbarton, Rangers, Cambuslang, Third Lanark, Hearts, Aberdeen, St Mirren, Vale of Leven and Cowlairs – and while the club from the East End of Glasgow were very much the new boys of Scottish football, having reached the final of the Scottish Cup in their very first season two years earlier, confidence was high at the original Celtic Park that they could make a proper challenge for the new piece of silverware.

The first time the name 'McMahon' appeared on a scoresheet for Celtic was on 11 April that same year in what was his sixth appearance for the club. A crowd of around 10,000 were at Celtic Park to witness the moment, though it's unlikely any of them would have appreciated the significance of the goal. Certainly, none of them could have predicted that McMahon would go on to score a total of 179 goals for the club in a thirteen-year period.

Dumbarton were the first opponents to feel the force of McMahon's scoring prowess though they certainly wouldn't be the last, and his goal proved to be the only one of the game, which was enough to give Celtic the victory. It was an impressive enough victory against a side who would only lose two games that season and who would be declared joint champions of 1890/91 along with Rangers after the two sides fought out a 2–2 play-off draw for the title.

Celtic, however, finished third in the league, eight points off the leaders, though this wasn't helped by the deduction of four points because of an infringement of the rules; they fielded an ineligible player, goalkeeper James Bell, at the beginning of the campaign when he wasn't fully cleared to play for the club.

McMahon scored six goals in that first season including an impressive *four* goals in the 9–1 victory over Vale of Leven in the second-last game of the campaign, though the 'Top Goalscorer of the Season' Award went to Peter Dowds, who netted 17 goals, including 15 in the league.

100TH GOAL

In his first season at the club, Sandy McMahon forced his way into the team and he began to establish his credentials as a goalscorer. He would enhance his reputation further over the next four seasons when he finished as Celtic's top scorer every year, during which time the club began to fill the trophy cabinet with some silverware: a Scottish Cup in 1892 and two league titles in 1893 and 1894.

His goal tally gradually mounted up and it was in season 1895/96 that McMahon scored his 100th goal for Celtic. It was a momentous occasion, though the history books record that a crowd of just 1,000 were at Celtic Park on 7 December 1895 to witness the goal, which came in a 2–1 victory over St Bernard's. The victory made up for the 3–0 defeat the Celts had suffered against the same team earlier in the season.

It was also a campaign which saw Celtic reclaim the league title, finishing four points clear of second-placed Rangers. In the 18-game season, the Celts lost just three games and in winning their final 11 matches in a row, they scored 49 goals, of which Sandy McMahon was responsible for 13.

However, he didn't finish as Celtic's top scorer that season, with Allan Martin, who had joined the club from Hibernian, hitting eighteen for the season – scoring three more than McMahon.

There were also a couple of notable scorelines in that impressive run of games; the very first 6–2 thrashing of Rangers, when McMahon scored twice, and the club's record victory, an 11–0 home win over Dundee, when the same player also chipped in with two goals.

In the game against St Bernard's on 7 December it was the opening goal which would be Sandy McMahon's 100th for the club. It was an impressive achievement for a player who had taken just five years to reach his century and, in the process, he also ensured a special place in Celtic's history as the first ever player to score 100 goals for the club. The magnitude of that achievement should not be under-estimated, particularly when you consider that only twenty-seven other players have managed to follow in McMahon's footsteps.

LAST GOAL

Sandy McMahon's final goal for Celtic – his 179th no less – came on 14 February 1903 in a first-round Scottish Cup tie against St Mirren. He was one of four scorers that day in a 4–0 victory for the Celts, though it was a second replay of the tie, the two previous games having finished 0–0 and 1–1.

He netted Celtic's third of the game in front of a crowd of 30,000, though just like the 1,000 who had witnessed his very first goal, none of the supporters that day would have realised they were celebrating a Sandy McMahon goal for the very last time or that over 100 years later, his goalscoring exploits would continue to be written about and remembered.

Two weeks after scoring that goal, McMahon played his final game for the club, in a Scottish Cup quarter-final tie against

Rangers at Celtic Park. Sadly, he wasn't able to bow out with a goal and Celtic could not provide him with the victory his illustrious career so richly deserved, as the visitors ran out 3–0 winners. It was another barren season for the club, who also finished fifth in the league, and McMahon wasn't able to add to the four league titles and three Scottish Cups he'd already won.

Sadly too, he finished his career just before Celtic embarked on a then world record run of six league titles in a row between 1905 and 1910, with Jimmy Quinn taking over as the leading goalscorer at the club during this time as another player who comfortably passed a century of goals, and who went on to score even more goals than Sandy McMahon.

HIGHS AND LOWS

Season 1891/92 saw the first major honour head to the East End of Glasgow when Celtic won the Scottish Cup. Sandy McMahon was enjoying his first full season at the club and would be the club's top scorer that season, netting twenty league goals and five in the cup. Two of those five goals came in the replay of the final against Queen's Park in a 5–1 victory.

Celtic had won the first game 1–0 but owing to a combination of circumstances – poor weather and crowd encroachment onto the pitch which caused frequent delays – a replay had been agreed during the match, though without the crowd being informed.

The replay was also played at Ibrox on 9 April 1892 and a crowd of 26,000 saw Celtic win the oldest trophy in world football for the very first time. McMahon netted Celtic's third and fifth goals of the game, with another Century Bhoy, Johnny Campbell, also grabbing a double, while Queen's Park chipped in with an own goal.

It was a famous victory for the fledgling club, and McMahon would help the club win two further Scottish Cups; in 1899, when they beat Rangers 2–0 and in 1900, when they beat Queen's Park 4–3. In both of those finals, McMahon also managed to get on the scoresheet.

In recent years, a 6–2 victory over Rangers has become one of the most famous in the club's history. Nicknamed the 'Demolition Derby', it heralded the dawn of the Martin O'Neill era and a period of domestic domination for Celtic.

Back in 1895/96, Celtic recorded their first 6–2 win over their rivals, and McMahon scored two of those six goals. In total, he scored sixteen goals against Rangers in League and Scottish Cup fixtures, while he also netted a hat-trick in a 4–0 victory against the Ibrox side on 25 May 1895 to help Celtic win the Glasgow Charity Cup.

The lowest point for the club, during the thirteen years that McMahon was there, came on 9 January 1897 when they were knocked out of the Scottish Cup by junior side, Arthurlie.

While McMahon would have felt the shock of the defeat as much as anyone at the club, from a personal point of view he would have been thankful that he wasn't in the team which lost 4–2.

He had been injured the week before the game, when Celtic were also without several other key players through injury, but a 'strike' by several of the players, objecting to press criticism of the team, saw some of them fail to appear for the game, including Dan Doyle, and the Celts started the game with just nine men.

Willie Maley later described it as:

probably the greatest sensation ever known in Scottish football. The section of the press which had contributed to disorganisation of the team owing to the strike was jubilant, but the more dignified organs were really sympathetic, knowing all the circumstances.

The following season the teams met again, and Celtic beat Arthurlie 7–0, with McMahon scoring two of the goals.

AND ANOTHER THING ...

While Sandy McMahon remained at the club until October 1903 when he joined Partick Thistle, one of the greatest players Celtic has ever produced never wore the famous green and white Hoops in a competitive game. He only played in the green and white stripes.

Celtic changed their strip to the Hoops at the start of season 1903/04 but McMahon had already played his last game for the club. For a player who can comfortably stake his claim to have been the first genuine Celtic legend, it's a pity that none of his exploits were in a strip that became famous throughout the footballing world and synonymous with free-flowing, attacking football – the Celtic way – and Sandy McMahon certainly played the game in that manner.

In an era of proper nicknames, rather than simply adding a 'y' to the end of a player's surname, McMahon was known as 'Duke'.

The origins of the moniker most likely lie with the former president of France, Patrice de Mac-Mahon, Duc de Magenta. It's claimed that when the former president died in October 1893, newspaper vendors in Glasgow tried to boost sales by proclaiming 'McMahon deid! McMahon deid!'

It seems likely that it was Tom Maley who gave Sandy McMahon the nickname of 'Duke', though he was also known as the 'Prince of Dribblers' by supporters, which gives an indication of his skill with a ball at his feet.

However, things would have turned out very differently had Nottingham Forest succeeded in luring McMahon to England.

They had already managed to capture Neilly McCallum, the scorer of Celtic's first ever goal in the 5–2 victory over Rangers back in 1888, and it was McCallum who tried to persuade McMahon to join him.

There followed all sorts of subterfuge, with the player being moved from hotel to hotel by Forest, all the while tracked by Celtic officials who eventually managed to talk McMahon into staying in Glasgow.

Willie Maley later set the story down in print, explaining that 'Celtic could stand for McCallum's defection, but McMahon, then at his best, was a "soo o' anither sort".'

Promptly messengers were secretly sent south, and after much trouble discovered that McMahon was being kept in the country in order to hold him safely until he committed himself to Notts Forest in a game on Saturday. The scouts discovered his lair but then found he had been taken into Nottingham for the day.

They followed there only to see him going back by a train on the opposite side of the arrival platform: once again to the country, they this time 'woo'ed' the Duke (as he was known by the football fans of his day) back to Scotland to play many wonderful games for the Celtic.

It is to the eternal gratitude of all Celtic supporters that Sandy McMahon was 'woo'ed' back to Glasgow, because Celtic Football Club would have been all the poorer without his contribution.

9

JIMMY McMENEMY

168 GOALS IN 515 GAMES

Jimmy McMenemy played for Celtic in an era when football players' nicknames often had a great deal of thought behind them. In the modern age, surnames of players tend to get a 'y' added on and that is pretty much it. Yet, back in the early 1900s, footballers were sometimes handed more original monikers. McMenemy's universal name was 'Napoleon', due to the fact he was viewed as a master of strategy. He was also a master of goalscoring.

Few Celtic players match McMenemy in terms of longevity. He joined the club in 1902 and stayed until 1920. He picked up a treasure chest of medals – 11 league titles and 6 Scottish Cups – and scored a total of 168 goals in his 515 competitive games. If Jimmy Quinn was the keystone of the first great Celtic team, then McMenemy wasn't far behind. Together, they were a potent force for Celtic.

When Celtic won six-in-a-row between 1905 and 1910, McMenemy was a huge inspiration. When four successive titles were secured between 1914 and 1917, he was again a creative fulcrum for Celtic. Napoleon could do everything a forward needed to. He had pace, unbelievable skill and a powerful shot, but he was also a calming presence on the pitch. Legend says that his trademark cry was 'Keep the heid' whenever games got a bit heated.

McMenemy experienced everything in the game over his eighteen-year Celtic career. He left the club as a player in 1920 but still had time to make an impact at Partick Thistle, helping them beat Rangers in the final of the 1921 Scottish Cup. After ten years out of the game, he became a coach at Partick Thistle before returning to Celtic in a similar capacity, where his experience was used to the full.

He is remembered as a Celtic icon; as a man who gave his all for the club for almost two decades and then returned as a coach help to mould a new Celtic team and again bring success to the club. Jimmy's heart never left Celtic Park and he lived to see Jock Stein's first trophy as manager. He had passed away by the time Celtic had conquered Europe, but that feat would not have surprised him. He always knew the club was destined for greatness.

FIRST GOAL

It's important to get off on the right foot at every new club. Jimmy McMenemy managed this with consummate ease by scoring on his Celtic debut against Port Glasgow on 22 November 1902. Celtic won 3–0 that day and those who witnessed this gifted young player score his first goal were watching the start of something special. Goals, however, were all well and good. What the Celtic supporters really wanted were trophies. McMenemy didn't disappoint in this respect.

Jimmy had officially signed for Celtic on 6 June 1902, but he had been on the club's list of potential targets for a lot longer. He played a trial match against Motherwell in 1900 before returning to the Juniors. By 1902, his progress was such that Celtic couldn't ignore him. Willie Maley gave him another trial, but Everton – like they would with Bobby Collins years later –

were also showing interest. Celtic eventually bit the bullet, made an offer and a star was born.

Maley was in the process of building a team to challenge for honours and McMenemy was an integral part of his plans. The 1904 Scottish Cup final triumph, with a show-stealing performance from Jimmy Quinn, was the first tangible sign that something special was unfolding at Celtic. Napoleon, playing inside-right in that game, was central to the club's dramatic success.

He had a similar influence on one of the most remarkable Glasgow derbies of all time, the play-off for the 1904/05 Scottish title. Celtic and Rangers had finished level on points and in those days there were no other methods of splitting the teams, barring a play-off. If goal difference had been used, Rangers would have been champions. Celtic had finished their league campaign on 4 March, but had to wait until 6 May to face Rangers in the play-off at Hampden Park.

After the controversy involving Jimmy Quinn's sending off in the previous derby, won by Rangers 2–0 in the Scottish Cup semi-final, an English referee was used in an attempt to dampen any tension. In the event, the game went off without a hitch and McMenemy got on the scoresheet as Celtic won 2–1 and started a run of six successive championships.

100TH GOAL

The story of six-in-a-row is a simple one. Willie Maley's Celtic side, with Jimmy McMenemy one of the stars, was unstoppable. Between 1905 and 1910, Celtic saw off all comers and even added two Scottish Cups to the collection. They were a fine side, with strength and quality in every area, and the other Scottish sides had no answer to their slick movement and clinical finishing.

McMenemy, while never finishing as the top marksman, was

the perfect foil for players like Jimmy Quinn, Peter Somers and David Hamilton. They all had their assets but McMenemy knitted it all together and the bulk of his first 100 goals came during that spell, as Celtic's first great team kept defying the odds to gain title after title. In a social sense, this success also gave the many Irish immigrants who followed the team something to be proud of.

The six-in-a-row side also achieved successive Scottish Cup triumphs in 1907 and 1908. They beat Hearts 3–0 in the first final and then, twelve months later, routed St Mirren 5–1. It could have been three-in-a-row but after Celtic drew against Rangers in the original final and replay, the cup was withdrawn following a riot in the second match.

Celtic's dominance finally ended in season 1910/11 and this was the campaign in which McMenemy scored his 100th goal for the club. It came on 10 December 1910, when Celtic beat Clyde 2–0 in an away match. Celtic were going for a seventh consecutive title but they ultimately came up short as Rangers halted their rivals' remarkable run.

LAST GOAL

Jimmy McMenemy's last goal for Celtic came on 6 December 1919, in a 5–0 home win over Motherwell. Napoleon scored twice in the rout. By that stage, he had won six titles in a row for Celtic between 1905 and 10 and another four titles in a row between 1913 and 17 and had brought numerous other cups back to Celtic Park. He had also retired briefly, before returning to a hero's welcome at his football home.

What can be said about the four-in-a-row run from 1914 to 1917? Well, quite simply, Willy Maley created another fantastic team and McMenemy played a starring role in it. Jimmy McColl,

John Browning, Andy McAtee and Patsy Gallacher were also stars of this wonderful Celtic side who gained success by playing in the best traditions of the club. After Rangers stopped Celtic's run, McMenemy got his hands on the league title one more time in 1919. It would prove to be his final triumph for Celtic.

After a spell at Partick Thistle, McMenemy's playing days were over but his influence on the game continued as he embarked on a successful coaching career, first at Partick Thistle and then Celtic. Napoleon was a master strategist on the pitch and he made his presence felt as a member of the club's backroom staff. It was in the autumn of 1934 that he returned and, less than two years later, the league title was secured in 1936. McMenemy's approach and aura seemed to get the best out of the players. He was once again a key figure within the club.

He was referred to as 'the trainer' and was a perfect sidekick to manager Willie Maley. McMenemy was responsible for the coaching and motivation during matches. He must have been doing something right as the trophies continued to flow in the pre-war years. In 1937, the Scottish Cup came home to Paradise and the Empire Exhibition Cup joined the league championship trophy in the 1938 team photo. McMenemy, after achieving so much as a player, felt immense pride as he helped write another glorious chapter in the club's history.

The war, of course, rendered football insignificant and McMenemy left Celtic in the period after Maley departed in 1940. In the next twenty-five years before his death, Napoleon watched Celtic regularly as a supporter. Few men gave more to the club than Jimmy McMenemy. Countless new chapters of Celtic's history have been written, but he remains an example to all who follow him. His longevity was quite extraordinary.

HIGHS AND LOWS

It was June 1918 and the Celtic supporters were in for a shock as news broke that Jimmy McMenemy was retiring. This icon, a man who had done so much for the club, had called time on his playing career. Naturally, this was a low point for McMenemy but, by December of the same year he was back in the fold, as he returned against Dumbarton. By the end of the season, Celtic were champions again.

Given that he won eleven league titles and six Scottish Cups in his eighteen years with the club and then led them to even more glory as a coach, it's hard to pick any real low points from McMenemy's time at Celtic, although the wisdom of his departure from the club in 1920 is suspect. He still had much to offer, despite his thirty-nine years. With his football brain, he could have easily played on for Celtic. Instead, he moved on and won a Scottish Cup with Partick Thistle.

If we are to pick specific highlights from McMenemy's time, then his role and goal in the 1905 league title decider against Rangers ranks among his finest moments. He loved playing against Rangers and save his best derby goal for a match on New Year's Day 1914. The last 100 years may have exaggerated the exact amount of defenders that lay in his wake as he savoured a spectacular strike, but at least four or five players were left for dead before he exploded his shot into the net. Celtic won that game 4–0.

Yet, it would be wrong to sum up the value of McMenemy in terms of merely goals and trophies. He was so much more to Celtic. He was a trailblazer and a faithful servant to the club. He helped Celtic break new ground and, between 1905 and 1919, helped the club win a staggering eleven league titles. That level of success is hugely impressive in any era.

AND ANOTHER THING ...

Jimmy McMenemy was capped twelve times by Scotland and scored five goals. Just like his Celtic career, his Scotland days spanned a lengthy time, fifteen years in total. He won his first cap against Northern Ireland in 1905 and won his last cap against Northern Ireland in 1920. Of the five goals he scored for Scotland, he scored three against Northern Ireland and two against England. In total, he played against England three times and never finished on the losing side, winning two and drawing one.

Oddly, for someone who regularly scored goals, Jimmy never once finished as Celtic's top scorer in a league season, although with Jimmy Quinn, Patsy Gallacher and Jimmy McColl around, that shouldn't be viewed as a criticism. During his Celtic career, he scored a total of four hat-tricks. All four came in league competition.

Football ran in the McMenemy family. The great Jimmy had two sons who also played football. John, also an attacker, played sixteen times for Celtic and scored two goals for the club between 1925 and 1928. He also played for Motherwell, Partick Thistle and St Mirren. John never made the impact his father did at Celtic, but he had some of his silky attributes on the pitch. Harry, another son of Jimmy, played for Newcastle United.

10

KENNY DALGLISH
167 GOALS IN 320 APPEARANCES

He had a smile which would light up a football stadium and a sense of joy in playing a sport that came naturally to him. He put the 'beautiful' into the game and, while others sweated and toiled and made the best of what ability they had, he danced and darted his way across the many fields of his dreams, inviting adulation from supporters who knew they were watching a unique footballing talent. Quite simply, Kenny Dalglish is one of the best players Scotland has ever produced and one of the greatest ever to grace the green and white Hoops.

Not that he took his God-given talent for granted. Far from it, Dalglish worked tirelessly throughout his playing career to be the best he possibly could. There is a sense, in looking back on that career, that he did indeed make the most of what he had and did not squander the gift he had. There are no 'what-ifs' in Kenny Dalglish's time as a player.

He was successful at Celtic, winning four league championships, four Scottish Cups and one League Cup before going on to replicate and perhaps even surpass that success with Liverpool, which included three European Cup triumphs. Add in the fact that he is Scotland's most capped player with 102 appearances for his country, and it's hard to imagine any other player being able to boast such a treasure trove of honours.

The 'what-ifs' would only be harboured by Celtic supporters

who idolised the player in the 1970s and mourned his departure in 1977. What if he had stayed? Would it have been Celtic who had triumphed in Europe? Would the club have enjoyed another period of domestic dominance? Would Jock Stein have stayed longer as manager?

The year when Dalglish headed south to Anfield saw Celtic lose their 'King Kenny', while the world lost the King of Rock 'n' Roll, when Elvis Presley died on 16 August, just six days after Dalglish left Glasgow. It sounds flippant to highlight which event devastated the Celtic fans more, but such is the nature of football.

There are countless reasons why Celtic as a club, and its supporters, should be thankful to Sean Fallon. The Sligo man was a faithful servant of the club as a player throughout the fallow 1950s, though he, along with every other supporter, enjoyed the unexpected triumph of the 7–1 League Cup final victory over Rangers as much as anyone.

Having played alongside Jock Stein for the Hoops, he would become Stein's trusted lieutenant in the dugout when he took over as Celtic manager and led the club to unparalleled success over the next few years.

Perhaps the most important reason to be thankful to Sean Fallon is that he was the man who persuaded Kenny Dalglish to sign for Celtic. Legend has it that the Irishman stopped at Dalglish's house on the way to the coast for a family day out with his wife and daughter, and while they waited in the car, he went inside to get the youngster's signature.

It was at least two hours later that he re-emerged, having had to use all his powers of persuasion to get the boy to put pen to paper. It was a triumph that he did, and Celtic would reap the benefits of that for the next few years, even if Fallon probably had to incur the immediate wrath of his family when he got back into the car that day.

Dalglish signed provisional forms with Celtic just three weeks before the club won the European Cup in 1967, though the season after that he was farmed out to junior side Cumbernauld United before becoming a full-time professional at the club in April 1968.

He joined a group of promising young players coming through the ranks at Celtic and, on the back of the European triumph, it did appear that the future was looking bright for the club. With the exception of Danny McGrain, none would be as successful at Celtic as Dalglish, though the latter would go on to even greater footballing heights elsewhere.

FIRST GOAL

Kenny Dalglish made his Celtic debut on 25 September 1968, coming on as a substitute for Charlie Gallagher in the League Cup quarter-final second leg against Hamilton at Douglas Park. He was seventeen years old.

Celtic knew they had unearthed a special footballing talent when Sean Fallon persuaded him to sign for the club, despite the fact he'd grown up as a Rangers fan. Just as importantly, Celtic had Jock Stein in charge and he was aware that this talent would need to be nurtured.

So, after his debut, Dalglish disappeared back into the reserves for the next three years, making only sporadic first-team appearances: four in 1969/70 and the same again the following season.

In the meantime, he honed his craft as part of the so-called 'Quality Street Gang'; the name given to the promising crop of young players who emerged in the immediate aftermath of Celtic's 1967 European Cup triumph. Alongside Dalglish, there was Danny McGrain, Davie Hay, George Connelly, Lou Macari and Vic Davidson.

The future looked bright for the club and the brightest star of all was Dalglish. He finally emerged at the beginning of 1971/72, scoring three times in three games against Rangers in the early stages of the season.

Two of those games were in the sectional stage of the League Cup, while the other was the second league game of the season. All of the matches were played at Ibrox because of ground reconstruction work at Celtic Park, and so it was that Kenny Dalglish scored his first goal for the club in a 'home' game at Ibrox on 14 August 1971.

Celtic won 2–0 that day, with Jimmy Johnstone opening the scoring on 67 minutes. Three minutes later, John Hughes was brought down in the box and the Hoops had a penalty. Despite an abundance of experience in the Celtic ranks, it was Dalglish who was nominated by his captain, Billy McNeill, to step forward, and the young player showed no sign of nerves as he duly despatched the spot-kick past goalkeeper Peter McCloy.

It was his first goal for Celtic and his first goal against Rangers, all wrapped up in one bundle and it quickly became obvious that Dalglish had developed a taste for scoring against the team he had once supported.

In the corresponding League Cup fixture, also played at Ibrox, he opened the scoring just after half-time as Celtic cruised to a 3–0 victory. And in the first league clash of the new campaign, he provided the equaliser after Celtic had gone 2—1 down, before Jimmy Johnstone scored a last-minute winner with a remarkable header.

Having nurtured Dalglish, Jock Stein now unleashed him and Dalglish played 50 of Celtic's 58 games that season, scoring 23 goals in the course of a campaign which saw the Hoops secure a league and Scottish Cup double.

100TH GOAL

It took Kenny Dalglish just over three years to score 100 goals for Celtic and the milestone goal arrived on 14 December 1974 at Dens Park. He netted a hat-trick that day and it was the third goal on seventy-one minutes which was also Dalglish's 100th in the Hoops.

Former Celtic striker John McPhail, writing in the *Celtic View* after that game, said:

> What a victory for Celtic at Dens Park on Saturday. And what a personal triumph for Kenny Dalglish. This young man has played many fine games in a Celtic jersey but I have no hesitation to rank this with the legendary displays by the heroes of the past. We called the 8–1 victory at Dens a few seasons ago the Jimmy Johnstone match. This, to all present, will always be remembered as the Kenny Dalglish game.

By the end of the year, Celtic were two points clear of Rangers at the top of the table as they attempted to secure an incredible tenth league title in a row. While 1975 kicked off with a 5–1 home victory over Clyde on 1 January, with Dalglish on the scoresheet, the 3–0 defeat just three days later at Ibrox signalled a catastrophic collapse that would see Celtic finish third in the table, eleven points behind Rangers in first place.

Of their fourteen league fixtures after the defeat to Rangers, Celtic won just four while they suffered an unprecedented seven defeats. It was an ignominious way to relinquish a title that had almost come to be seen as the property of the club since 1966, and the manner of the loss was completely unexpected.

The team had already lifted the League Cup in October with a 6–3 victory over Hibernian in the final, which featured a Dixie

Deans hat-trick, and they would go on to lift the Scottish Cup at the end of the season with a 3–1 win over Airdrie. That game is remembered more for the fact it was the last competitive match Billy McNeill, the captain of the Lisbon Lions, played for the club, having amassed an incredible total of 790 appearances since making his debut in August 1958.

Dalglish scored twenty-one goals that season, one less than top scorer Paul Wilson who, remarkably, had played in the Scottish Cup final and scored two of the goals just a couple of days after the death of his mother.

Season 1974/75 marked the end of the Scottish First Division in its eighteen-team format, which had been the case for the previous twenty years. Prior to that, the number of teams in the top division had fluctuated between sixteen, eighteen or twenty, but not since the earliest days of the league had Scotland's top domestic trophy been competed for by only ten teams.

That was the case going into 1975/76 with the inception of the Scottish Premier Division, which featured the clubs who'd finished in the top ten the previous season, and Celtic kicked off the campaign with a visit to Ibrox where they lost 2–1, Dalglish opening the scoring just before half-time for the Hoops, who conceded two second-half goals.

The new format of the league saw teams playing each other four times in the course of the season, and Celtic failed to beat Rangers in any of their meetings, drawing both matches at home and losing at Ibrox in the Ne'erday fixture. Not surprisingly, it was Rangers who lifted the title that season, finishing six points clear of Celtic.

Dalglish was once again the top scorer at the club, hitting an impressive thirty-two goals in all competition, but it was Celtic's first season without a trophy since 1963/64, though there's no doubt that the absence of Jock Stein from the dugout for the whole of that campaign, as he recovered from the serious injuries sustained in a car crash, had a profound effect on the club and what was a disappointing season.

LAST GOAL

Celtic had already secured the Double by the time they faced Motherwell at Fir Park in the final league fixture of the campaign. The match came just three days after the 1–0 victory over Rangers in the Scottish Cup final, when an Andy Lynch penalty was enough to give Celtic the trophy, and it may well have been a Hampden hangover which saw the home side take a 2–0 lead in the first-half.

Whatever the reason for it was, Jock Stein's half-time team-talk seemed to galvanise the Hoops and they scored twice after the break to take a share of the points.

Dalglish's goal – his 167th for the club – came in the sixty-ninth minute, though it had been preceded nine minutes earlier by Tommy Burns' first ever goal for the club.

On the back of winning the League and Scottish Cup, optimism at Celtic Park was as high as it had been for a considerable time. Jock Stein appeared to have recovered fully from the car crash which had almost killed him, and he appeared to be relishing the opportunity to build another successful Celtic side, and perhaps era? The triumvirate who would lead the club to new glories were Kenny Dalglish, Danny McGrain and Pat Stanton, three world-class players who had been outstanding in the double-winning season.

Sadly, and it seemed like it happened in the blink of an eye, Stein was deprived of the services of all three: McGrain suffered an ankle injury that would rule him out for eighteen months; Stanton suffered a knee injury in the first game of the season against Dundee United and never played again; and Kenny Dalglish left the club to join Liverpool.

The cumulative effect of losing the three best players in the team at the same time saw Celtic finish an unprecedented fifth in the league, their lowest position in thirteen years, and it heralded the end of Jock Stein's reign at Celtic. For a man who had taken Celtic to incredible heights at home and in Europe, amassing ten league titles, eight Scottish Cups, six League Cups and, of course, the European Cup in 1967, it was an ignominious end to his time as Celtic manager, though it could never diminish his achievements.

Luck deserted Stein that last season when he would have been relishing the challenge of retaining the league title and venturing into the European Cup once again.

Dalglish not only went on to play in the same competition but he also lifted the trophy at the end of the season, scoring the only goal of the game at Wembley to beat Brugge and ensure Liverpool retained the trophy they'd won for the first time the previous season. It was a painful reminder to Celtic supporters of what they had lost. Kenny Dalglish was a world-class player. They had always known that and now, so did the rest of Europe. Unfortunately, it was not in the green and white Hoops of Celtic but the red of Liverpool that he would scale the heights of Europe.

HIGHS AND LOWS

Kenny Dalglish won nine trophies during the ten years he was at Celtic, but he was never fortunate enough to play in a European Cup final for the club. He'd signed provisional forms with the club a few weeks before the 1967 triumph in Lisbon and hadn't yet managed to break through to the first-team squad by the time they reached the final in Milan three years later, though that game ended in a disappointing extra-time defeat to Feyenoord.

There were two semi-finals: against Inter Milan in 1972 when

Celtic lost on penalties; and two years later, against Atlético Madrid, who won the tie 2–0 on aggregate.

That only tells a fraction of the story and doesn't take into account Atlético's shameful performance in the first leg at Celtic Park when three players were sent off and eight booked as the Madrid players assaulted their Celtic opponents throughout the match. The frustrations of the home side boiled over with a mass brawl in the tunnel at the end of the game. Atlético reached the final when they should have been thrown out of the competition, and Celtic have yet to reach the last four of that tournament since.

It was perhaps a desire to play again and succeed at that level, which made Dalglish join Liverpool, who were the reigning European champions in 1977, over and above any financial incentives that were undoubtedly there in moving to England. Several of his contemporaries had already done so, most notably Lou Macari and Davie Hay, who joined Manchester United and Chelsea respectively, but none were as successful as Dalglish.

In ten years at Celtic, he scored enough goals to put him in the top ten of all-time greatest goalscorers at the club and, in the intervening period, only Henrik Larsson has scored more goals in the Hoops than Kenny Dalglish.

AND ANOTHER THING ...

Kenny Dalglish's connection with Celtic didn't end the day he left in 1977, though it was over twenty years later before formal links with the club were restored. In June 1999, he returned to Celtic Park as Director of Football with his former Liverpool teammate, John Barnes, appointed as head coach. It was heralded at the time as the 'dream team', with Dalglish's managerial experience complimenting Barnes' lack of it.

Dalglish had stepped effortlessly into management, first guiding Liverpool to the Double as player-manager before eventually hanging up his boots in May 1990, by which time he had won three league titles and two FA Cups with the Anfield side.

During that time, he was also in charge when Liverpool and its supporters suffered the almost unimaginable tragedy of Hillsborough on 15 April 1989 when ninety-six Liverpool fans lost their lives during an FA Cup semi-final.

Dalglish's dignity and the manner of his leadership during that terrible time impressed everyone and remains a measure of the man.

He left Liverpool in 1991 and though it appeared initially that he wanted, and needed, a break from football, six weeks later he was appointed Blackburn Rovers' manager, eventually guiding them to the Premiership title in 1995. Two years later, he took over at Newcastle United, guiding them to runners-up spot in the Premiership, and so, by the time he joined Celtic in 1999, he had a wealth of experience and success to bring to the club and which John Barnes could call upon.

Sadly, the 'dream team' didn't work out at Celtic, and Barnes was sacked in February 2000, after the shock Scottish Cup exit at the hands of Inverness Caley Thistle.

Dalglish took over the managerial reigns in the short-term, bringing in Tommy Burns to assist him, and they managed to win the League Cup that season, beating Aberdeen 2–0 in the final.

11

ADAM McLEAN

148 GOALS IN 408 APPEARANCES

Great Celtic goalscorers have always needed wingers to supply chances. Talk to the modern striking greats like Henrik Larsson and John Hartson and they will tell you that they wouldn't have scored half of their goals had the likes of Alan Thompson, Lubo Moravcik, Didier Agathe, Steve Guppy, Shaun Maloney and Aiden McGeady not been around. For Hartson and Larsson, these men were the creative foils, the players who would produce that moment of magic to create some pace and let the strikers finish off the job.

Jimmy McGrory remains Celtic's most prolific scorer of all time, yet there must have been players who, time after time, would give the legendary striker the platform on which to showcase his talents; players who would do the build-up work and let McGrory do the rest. Of course, there were such players and no one did more to aid McGrory in his scoring feats than Adam McLean. Yet what set McLean apart from most other Celtic wingers was his unerring ability to find the net as well. His record of 148 goals and countless more assists shows that, crucially, there was a real end product to his play and that was an invaluable asset for Celtic at that time.

McLean won his fair share of silverware – four league titles and three Scottish Cups – and remained a consistent scorer during his entire Celtic career. It took him a few months to get off and running but he soon became a goal-getter of some repute. When he wasn't feeding McGrory with another inch-perfect cross, he often missed out the middle man and just scored himself. McLean, at times, was simply unplayable; a potent weapon in Celtic's attack.

Was he the greatest left winger in Celtic's history? Many observers and historians would say 'yes' to that question. While Jimmy Johnstone is incomparable on the right flank, McLean's delivery from wide areas and his knack for scoring goals, and plenty of them, puts him ahead of the many left wingers who came before and after him in green and white. He left Celtic under something of a cloud but, if anything, his departure crystallised just how much of an influence he had on the club. A favourite at every club he represented during his distinguished career, McLean made the most of his gift. He died in June 1973 but will be remembered as a Celtic Great.

FIRST GOAL

January 1917. A new year dawned at Celtic Park and Adam McLean was the name being talked about by the club's power-brokers. All the chat was about a winger who could score goals, someone who had all the ability and characteristics to be a success at Celtic. McLean didn't have the usual upbringing. Born in Greenock, he spent much of his youth living in Belfast but returned to his hometown and immediately displayed real talent on the football pitch. He was a stand-out for his juvenile team, Anderston Thornbank, and was destined for the top. Celtic got his signature and he joined on 17 January 1917.

Initially a centre forward, Willie Maley saw something different in McLean and asked if he wouldn't mind operating on the left wing as part of an experiment. McLean never looked back. His debut came against Dumbarton three days after he'd signed. Celtic drew 1–1 that day and McLean didn't score. That honour fell to Jimmy McColl. McLean would have to wait a while for that first Celtic goal.

Indeed, it wasn't until 28 April 1917, that McLean finally broke his duck with a goal in the 5–0 hammering of Clyde. That was Celtic's last game of the triumphant 1916/17 league campaign but McLean had served notice of his talents. The Celtic supporters wouldn't have known this at the time, but this young winger who looked so assured on the ball and had already demonstrated an eye for a goal, was going to become a vital cog in Maley's Celtic machine.

100TH GOAL

Almost nine years to the day since he had first walked into Celtic Park as a teenage wannabe, Adam McLean entered Celtic folklore with his 100th goal for the club. It came in the midst of another title-winning season for Celtic, with the Bhoys finishing eight points ahead of Airdrie come the end of the season. Sadly, it would prove to be McLean's last championship win for Celtic.

His century-clinching goal came against Queen's Park on 2 January 1926. Celtic won 4–1 that day and Jimmy McGrory scored twice, while Alex Thomson added the other goal. McGrory would go on to score 36 of Celtic's 97 league goals that season, many of which were set up by McLean, as Celtic comfortably clinched the title. Yet, there would be heartache for McLean in the Scottish Cup.

The winger had scored three goals as Celtic marched towards the last four but injury struck and McLean missed both the semi-final against Aberdeen and the final against St Mirren. His absence was a hammer-blow to Celtic, there is no other way to describe it. Without his guile, class and goal threat, Celtic were a weaker side and the Paisley men won the cup with a 2–0 win. McLean could only look on in anguish as St Mirren celebrated their Scottish Cup win.

LAST GOAL

It remains a crying shame that Adam McLean left Celtic in 1928. He was only twenty-nine and still had so much to offer, but it appears the decision to let him go was not made purely for football reasons. Some ninety years on, we can't say for sure, but the history books suggest that the Celtic hierarchy were not acting in the best interests of the club when they offered him reduced terms for season 1928/29.

Why did they do that? McLean's role as team spokesman prior to the USA tour of 1928 probably didn't help. He argued that conditions for the trip were not fair to the players. McLean, when contract talks began, then found the new deal was not to his liking. Celtic wouldn't budge and McLean, well within his rights, refused to sign the contract, although he later revealed, 'I didn't want to go.' Naturally, there was no shortage of interest and he travelled south to team up with his old partner in crime Tommy McInally at Sunderland. It was Celtic's loss. In fact, that's an understatement. It was an act of folly that deprived Celtic of at least four more years of a fantastic player.

McLean lasted two seasons at Sunderland before returning north to sign for Aberdeen in 1930. Three years later, he began a long association with Partick Thistle that saw him fill a variety of roles until the early 1960s. Throughout that spell, Celtic continued a fruitless search for a suitable replacement. They never found one. McLean's last goal came against St Johnstone on 18 April 1928. Celtic won 3–0 that day, the only victory of the last five league matches of the season, as Rangers won the title by five points. McLean's last goal also came just four days after Rangers had humbled Celtic 4–0 in a derby Scottish Cup final.

HIGHS AND LOWS

Adam McLean deserves to be remembered as a Celtic Great and thankfully he has the medals to back up that status. He played his part in four league championships – 1917, 1919, 1922 and 1926 – and also won three Scottish Cups, in 1923, 1925 and 1927. Those cup finals were special for Celtic, as always. Hibernian were beaten 1–0 in 1923 by a Joe Cassidy goal, while James McGrory and Patsy Gallacher were on target in 1925 as Dundee were beaten 2–1. McLean finally broke his Scottish Cup duck with a goal in the 3–1 win over East Fife in 1927.

Missing the 1926 Scottish Cup final was a huge blow for McLean, especially as he loved the open plains of Hampden and the thrill of playing for trophies on cup final day. To be deprived of that experience hit McLean hard. Yet, his darkest day came when he walked out of Celtic Park for the last time in 1928, predominately because he had no desire to leave the club at all. In hindsight, it was a huge misjudgement by the club.

AND ANOTHER THING ...

Adam McLean is widely regarded by Celtic historians as the best left winger ever to play for the club. Jimmy McMenemy, another Century Bhoy, concurs with that statement and named him in his all-time Celtic XI. His main strengths were skill, pace and dribbling technique; everything you would want in a winger. McLean's goals just added to the whole package.

Some people who didn't rate McLean that highly were the Scotland selectors. It seems criminal that he won only four caps for his country, although the famous Rangers winger Alan Morton was also deserving of a place in the national team during that era, and the selectors couldn't find space for both. Was McLean better than Morton? There's a debate to stoke the historical flames. Both had their assets, both were top-class players. McLean probably just shades it.

There's a wonderful Celtic anecdote about McLean, concerning his first visit to the stadium for his debut against Dumbarton. 'Report to the stadium,' he was told. No information about an entrance or anything. Just a simple, 'Report to the stadium.' Understandably, McLean looked like a lost soul as he searched for the right door but before long a voice boomed out, 'Whit's yer name son?' McLean responded as requested. 'Found him,' said the voice, which belonged to Jerry Reynolds, the former Celtic fullback. McLean was pointed towards Willie Maley who waited to greet him. The rest is Celtic history.

12

WILLIE WALLACE

134 GOALS IN 232 APPEARANCES

Willie Wallace was no fresh-faced youth when he signed for Celtic in December 1966. The striker was twenty-six years old and had been in the game since joining Stenhousemuir in 1958. He was already a League Cup winner with Hearts, while the Tynecastle side had narrowly missed out on winning the league in 1965, losing on goal average to Kilmarnock.

What made it all the more galling was the fact Hearts had scored 90 goals compared to Killie's 62, and if it had been decided on goal difference, the title would have headed to Edinburgh.

So Jock Stein's decision to bring the player to Celtic Park made a lot of football sense, although it may well have puzzled some supporters, given the firepower already at the Celtic manager's disposal. Stevie Chalmers, Bobby Lennox, Joe McBride and John Hughes were there, while the likes of Bobby Murdoch, Bertie Auld and Jimmy Johnstone contributed their fair share of goals, but Wallace not only augmented Stein's attacking options, but established his own place within that great group of players.

He had, to a certain extent, been rescued by Stein following a dispute between the player and Hearts.

'I was trying to get to Canada but I couldn't get away from Hearts,' Wallace explained.

I played without a contract for two years. As long as they had your registration there was nothing you could do about it as they owned you.

In fact, the way we got round it was to go back to one of the old slave laws to get rid of the retention, because that was what the wording was in the contract, you were 'retained'. Of course, legally nobody could do that as it was illegal to retain somebody.

With the path to Canada effectively blocked, the next logical step for the striker was a move down south. If he had got his own way, he could have been teaming up with fellow Scottish internationalist Bobby Moncur at St James' Park or leading a line fed from the back by recent World Cup-winning keeper Gordon Banks – until fate in the shape of Jock Stein stepped in.

'I spoke with both Newcastle and Stoke just before I was transferred to Celtic and both English clubs offered a lot more money,' Wallace recalled.

I don't even know what happened in the transfer dealing because we players never knew what went on in the boardroom or with the management.

You just took the deal or you didn't. As for Stoke and Newcastle, it was up to the club back then. Today the player would choose, but back then, I was sold and that was it and I wouldn't have a clue as to the reasoning. Both English sides were offering £80,000 and according to the press I came here for £28,000. It's always been a mystery to me.

Whatever the mystery, Stein had his man and what a man he proved to be, scoring 134 goals for the club over the next five years, and guaranteeing his place in the pantheon of Celtic legends.

FIRST GOAL

Jock Stein had signed Willie Wallace from Hearts on 6 December 1966 and just eleven days later he opened his scoring account for his new club, scoring twice in the 6–2 thrashing of Partick Thistle at Celtic Park. His first goal came after just two minutes. Bertie Auld crossed for Joe McBride who headed back across goal for Wallace to head home.

Writing in the *Celtic View* the following week, Jock Stein said: 'Willie Wallace has made a fine start with the club. Stevie Chalmers seems to have profited through his introduction, for Stevie has scored five goals in the two games in which Willie has taken part.'

Wallace had already made his debut in the Hoops, playing the previous week in a 4–2 home win over Motherwell when Chalmers netted a hat-trick.

It would be a season when Celtic couldn't stop scoring. They netted 111 and that was only in the league and Wallace, along with Chalmers, Joe McBride and Bobby Lennox, would spearhead that goalscoring threat in what was one of the most potent strike forces ever assembled in Scottish football.

Observers at the time speculated as to who he might replace in the Celtic starting XI, with most believing that it would be Chalmers, as the oldest of the forwards, who would make way for Wallace. In the event, it would be an injury to another key player, Joe McBride, which would provide an opening for Wallace in the team.

In saying that, Stein had used all his strikers in the game against Thistle when Wallace scored his first goal for the club, with Chalmers scoring twice and McBride also getting on the scoresheet. And the trio, along with Bobby Lennox, kept their places for the game on Christmas Eve at Pittodrie when McBride sustained the knee injury which effectively ended his season.

It was a cruel blow for a player in such a rich vein of goalscoring form – he would still end the season with thirty-five goals, only one behind Chalmers despite only playing for half the season, and it remains a point of speculation and debate among supporters as to what the starting line-up would have been at the European Cup final in Lisbon had McBride been fit. While there might be disagreements over the identities of all eleven, most are agreed on one thing – Joe McBride would have been in the team.

Whatever Stein's thoughts might have been, he had bought a player who already had a wealth of experience, including five years at Hearts and a couple of Scotland caps as well.

He would score 21 goals in the all-conquering 1966/67 season, and very quickly had a full set of medals to boast of, having already won the League Cup with Hearts in 1963. More medals and goals were to follow over the next few seasons.

100TH GOAL

It would be on the European stage that Willie Wallace would enjoy some of the finest moments of his career, given Celtic's sudden elevation into the top tier of European sides after 1967. So it should come as little surprise that his 100th goal for the club should have come in this environment.

The high of 1967 had been followed by the disappointing first-round exit the following season at the hands of Dynamo Kiev, and losing narrowly to AC Milan the year after that. Season 1969/70 would provide another opportunity for Celtic to claim Europe's top footballing prize, though ultimately it would end in cruel disappointment.

Having seen off FC Basel and Benfica, the latter by virtue of winning a toss of the coin after a 3–3 aggregate finish to the tie,

Celtic faced Italian champions Fiorentina in the quarter-final of the European Cup.

The first leg at Celtic Park attracted a crowd of around 80,000, and they witnessed a footballing master-class from Jock Stein's side, who were well worthy of the 3–0 scoreline at the end of the game. Bertie Auld gave the Hoops a first-half lead before an own goal just after the break put Celtic in command.

The third goal didn't come until the last minute of the match, and in scoring it Willie Wallace also became a bona fide Century Bhoy. He headed home from a Harry Hood cross to put Celtic in command in the tie and, despite a 1–0 defeat in Italy, it was Celtic who progressed to the semi-final of the competition and the proverbial 'Battle of Britain' clash against English champions Leeds United.

Wallace scored 13 European goals for Celtic, and undoubtedly the two he scored against Dukla Prague in the 1967 semi-final first leg at Celtic Park were the most important, but the goal against Fiorentina, his 100th for the Hoops, gave the team a cushion for the return leg in Florence where, despite a lot of pressure by the home side, they managed to emerge successfully from the tie.

They would also negotiate their way past Leeds in the semi-final, winning 3–1 on aggregate, although Wallace would miss the return leg at Hampden in front of European record attendance of 136,505, a late training injury ruling him out of the game.

He would return for the final against Feyenoord in Milan, however, but was left as disappointed as the rest of his Celtic teammates as they went down 2–1 in extra-time to the Dutch champions, missing out on the chance of a second European Cup triumph.

LAST GOAL

Europe also provided the platform for Willie Wallace's last goal for Celtic and it came just over a month before he left the club for Crystal Palace in a transfer that also saw John 'Yogi' Hughes move to Selhurst Park.

It was the first round, second-leg tie against BK 1903 Copenhagen, and the Danish side had shocked Celtic, along with the rest of Europe, by winning the first match 2–1. Natural order was restored in the return game, however, with a 3–0 victory for Celtic that came courtesy of two Willie Wallace goals and one from Tommy Callaghan.

Wallace opened the scoring on twenty-three minutes, but it was not until eleven minutes from time that Callaghan added a second. The final goal of the night, which would also be Wallace's last for the Hoops, came five minutes from time to ensure that it would be Celtic in the next round of the competition.

They would go on to reach the last four that season before losing out on penalties to Inter Milan after both ties finished goalless, but by then Wallace was plying his trade in England.

His last game for Celtic came on 2 October 1971, in a home league match against St Johnstone, and it wasn't the best way for him to bow out as Celtic lost the match 1–0. Whether Wallace realised at the time that it would be his last game for the club is debatable, and certainly the 38,000 fans who came along to Celtic Park that day would have given the player a rousing farewell in appreciation for his contribution to the cause.

He moved to Crystal Palace but returned to Scotland a year later, joining Dumbarton where, in the twilight of his career, he played alongside a youngster who would go on to forge an impressive career of his own in the Hoops, Murdo MacLeod.

Willie Wallace had proved to be a superb signing for Celtic, scoring 134 goals in 232 games, and he joined his fellow Celts at the time – Lennox, Chalmers, Hughes, Johnstone and Murdoch – in surpassing 100 goals in the Hoops. He is the club's twelfth top goalscorer of all time and can rightly be regarded as a Celtic Great.

HIGHS AND LOWS

'Show us your medals!' It's not a phrase recommended to be directed at any of the Celtic players from that golden period of Jock Stein's reign. Willie Wallace won five league titles with the club, along with three Scottish Cups, two League Cups and the European Cup. His only major disappointment was the 1970 European Cup final defeat to Feyenoord.

He arrived at the club in December 1966 and almost instantly became part of the goalscoring machine that Jock Stein had assembled for Celtic at that time. In the all-conquering 1966/67 season, he scored the two goals against Aberdeen which won the Scottish Cup.

That double at Hampden came just over two weeks after he'd scored two of the goals against Dukla Prague which gave Celtic a 3–1 first-leg lead in the semi-final of the European Cup. Indeed, he might even have had a hat-trick that night but for the crossbar, which denied him after he'd got on the end of a Stevie Chalmers cross. As it was, the victory was enough to see Celtic reach the final.

The game against the Czech side was also Wallace's first European appearance for the club and he could hardly have made a better mark on this stage.

As the Hoops blazed a trail across Europe, the players who wore the green and white Hoops were forging their own reputations in the game as a result. And it was a platform the players relished. Wallace later recalled:

I had been sitting beside the injured Joe McBride in the stand at Celtic Park to witness the astounding quarter-final against Vojvodina and I thought 'Wispy, this is the place for you.'

I wanted a slice of that, believe me. I know all the lads would say the same thing, but the atmosphere generated by our support on those occasions was just breathtaking … quite staggering really.

He was the club's top goalscorer in back-to-back seasons, 1968/69 and 1969/70, while even in his last full season, 1970/71, he still managed to net 28 goals in all competitions, bettered only by Harry Hood with 33.

AND ANOTHER THING …

Willie Wallace played his part in a 3–1 League Cup section victory over Rangers on 30 August 1967, at Celtic Park. The Hoops needed to win to make sure they finished top of the section and qualify for the quarter-final of the competition, but with twelve minutes of the match remaining, they were trailing 1–0.

Then Wallace stepped forward and provided one of three goals in a blistering end to the match. In the immediate aftermath of the game, Jock Stein proclaimed it the greatest victory in his time in charge at Celtic, no small boast considering that, just two months previously, his team had beaten Inter Milan 2–1 to win the European Cup.

Writing in the following week's *Celtic View*, however, the Celtic manager attempted to qualify his comments:

First of all, I did not make such a remark out of any feeling of relief that Celtic had won; we shall beat Rangers again in the future and they will beat us.

It was the manner of the victory last Wednesday night, the fact we won convincingly in circumstances that seemed very much against us, and on an occasion in which lesser players than Celtic's might have become despondent long before the end that led me to speak so highly of our success.

But when all the circumstances are taken into account, one victory over Rangers does not compare with beating teams like Dynamo Kiev and Inter Milan ... and Real Madrid in Spain.

Willie Wallace had been trying to extricate himself from his contract at Hearts in order to move to Canada when Celtic came calling in 1966, but the player still retained a desire to move further afield. The opportunity duly arrived in 1975 when he joined Apia in Sydney, Australia. He returned to Scotland two years later, but moved back to Australia in 1980, where he not only began working but also set up home, and it's in that country that he remains to this day.

13

JIMMY JOHNSTONE

130 GOALS IN 515 GAMES

All great football teams that have dominated eras and broken down barriers with their achievements have based their success on a collective effort. Look at the iconic football sides from history, Real Madrid from the 1960s, Ajax from the 1970s, AC Milan in the 1980s and early 1990s and Barcelona more recently, and you will find that they all functioned as a cohesive, effective unit. Yet, there is always room for a maverick, for a superstar who – while contributing to the team ethic – had the ability to change the entire flow of a game with a moment of individual brilliance.

The great Real Madrid side had Alfredo Di Stefano, Ajax had Johan Cruyff, while AC Milan relied heavily on the supreme striking prowess of Marco van Basten. Barcelona, in the modern age, have a collection of superstars, but Lionel Messi is first among equals. All of these world-class players had that extra spark, that inherent ability to produce something extraordinary on the biggest stage. For the Lisbon Lions, Jimmy Johnstone was that man. He was a unique talent; entertaining, effective and inspirational. He was also Celtic's greatest-ever player.

There was nothing simple about Johnstone. His talent was unique, off the cuff. He would beat defenders time and again. Then he would go back and do it all over again. Jimmy was the ultimate free spirit. He was a man who could light up a football pitch. The supporters loved him, his teammates loved him and

Jock Stein, while facing an ongoing battle to keep his star man on the straight and narrow, adored him. No other player in Celtic's history has been so universally loved and it was no surprise that the club's supporters voted him as the Greatest Ever Celt in 2002. 'I'm delighted. To be part of this is brilliant,' he said afterwards. Kenny Dalglish, who played with 'Jinky' and ran him close for the award, summed up his qualities: 'The wee man had everything, unbelievable skills and the heart of a lion.'

Johnstone won nineteen major honours for Celtic. He lifted nine league championships, four Scottish Cups and five League Cups. He was at his inspirational best as Celtic beat Inter Milan in the final of the 1967 European Cup. He created countless goals during Celtic's most productive era but he also scored his fair share and that's what sets him apart. Jimmy was the archetypal *tanner ba'* player but when a chance arose, he rarely messed about. For a winger, his record of 130 goals in 515 games is exceptional. Not only that, he scored in big games: derbies, league deciders, cup finals and huge European ties. For a small man, he was good in the air, while he often showed the instincts of a poacher. His long-range strike against Rangers to clinch the 1967 league title at Ibrox will go down as one of the best Celtic goals of all time.

In 2001, he was diagnosed with Motor Neurone Disease. It was the biggest battle he had ever faced and the world's admiration for Jimmy heightened as he bravely fought the illness and did everything in his power to raise awareness of it as he helped with fundraising efforts. His health deteriorated over the next five years and, tragically, he passed away on 13 March 2006. Celtic Park was turned into a shrine as fans from all over the world flocked to pay tribute to their favourite son.

As the funeral cortege passed by the stadium, the crowed offered an impromptu rendition of 'Jimmy Johnstone on the wing'. It was a poignant, emotional moment that perfectly encapsulated the indelible mark Jinky left on Celtic and everyone associated with the club. He is immortalised in a statue outside Celtic Park and not a day goes past without his memory being honoured. Celtic will probably never see the likes of Jimmy Johnstone again, but his legacy will live on forever.

FIRST GOAL

James Johnstone sat transfixed by the television set as a wing wizard by the name of Stanley Matthews ran amok at Wembley as his Blackpool side came from 3–1 down to beat Bolton 4–3 in the 1953 FA Cup final. It became known as the 'Matthews Final' and was a turning point in young Jimmy's life. From then on, he wanted to be like Stanley Matthews. He wanted to be the wing wizard. He got his wish through natural talent and hard work.

Given his size – Jimmy peaked at 5ft 4in – he would never have made a good centre half, so life as a winger was always going to suit him. Yet, Johnstone spent hours honing his skills and improving his speed and strength. If he was going to cope against bigger, rougher defenders, he was going to have to ensure that he was giving himself the best possible chance. He spent hours dribbling a ball through a succession of milk bottles and was forever doing weights and press-ups to increase his upper body strength.

In terms of talent, Johnstone had little to worry about. He was christened 'Jinky' because he was at his best jinking in between defenders. Where there was no space, he found some. From an early age, he would drop a shoulder, flick the ball with the outside of his boot and be away. Defenders didn't know what was coming and people started to notice his talent.

While still at school, one of Jimmy's teachers, Tommy Cassidy, told his friend Sammy Wilson, the Celtic player, that he had a talent on his hands. Jimmy was invited into the stadium and became a ball boy, where he would rub shoulders with Celtic players like Bobby Evans and Bobby Collins. They were heroes of Jimmy's but this job as a Celtic ball boy prevented him from playing every Saturday, so he cut it short and returned to Boys' Guild football with St Columba's. Soon, Manchester United showed interest but Celtic weren't going to sit by and let this precocious talent slip through the net. He signed an s-form and after being farmed out to Blantyre Juniors, he officially joined Celtic in November 1961.

Jimmy's debut was a moment to forget. He was part of a Celtic side that lost 6–0 to Kilmarnock at Rugby Park on 27 March 1963. Of the Celtic team that day, only Stevie Chalmers would join Johnstone in the European Cup-winning side four years later. Jimmy's first goal for Celtic came in April 1963 in a 4–3 defeat against Hearts at Tynecastle, but he had done enough to earn a place in the Celtic team to face Rangers in the Scottish Cup final. Jimmy played well in the 1–1 draw but didn't do enough to secure his place in the replay as Celtic lost 3–0.

A few months into the next season, 1963/64, Jimmy had become a first-team regular for Celtic and excelled on the European stage as the club reached the semi-final of the Cup-Winners' Cup. MTK Hungaria were Celtic's opponents and Johnstone scored in a 3–0 first-leg home win. However, a 4–0 defeat in Budapest ended Celtic's hopes of a place in the final and it was clear that Celtic had much to learn in the European arena. The arrival of Jock Stein ensured that wouldn't be a problem.

100TH GOAL

Jimmy Johnstone was a European champion by the time he scored his 100th goal for Celtic. It came on 18 December 1971, against Motherwell in a 5–1 rout at Fir Park and the image of him scoring a goal and running away before leaping into the air was etched into the minds of Celtic supporters all over the world. Jimmy also made a point of shaking the hands of his teammates whenever he scored. It was a subtle touch that showed, for all he was viewed as an individual, he knew the value of the team effort.

By 1971, Celtic were in the midst of a phenomenal period in the club's history. Trophies were arriving with impressive regularity. Jock Stein's team was becoming a hybrid of the Lisbon Lions and the Quality Street Gang, with a few aces thrown into the pack. Johnstone was a constant presence on the right wing and had added experience to the guile he always possessed.

In 1971/72, Celtic – as they always did at that time – won the league but were humbled 4–1 in the League Cup final by Partick Thistle and lost out on penalties to Inter Milan in the European Cup semi-final. Johnstone played in both games but there was some consolation when Celtic thumped Hibernian 6–1 in the Scottish Cup final. Jimmy, naturally, was outstanding.

He always loved cup finals. He loved the occasion and the sense of anticipation that it brought. Those showpiece games brought out the best in Jimmy. In 1967, he was lucky enough to play in what were virtually three cup finals in a matter of weeks. On 29 April, he was at his mesmerising best as Willie Wallace's two goals gave Celtic a 2–0 win over Aberdeen in the Scottish Cup final. Just a week later, he excelled with two magical goals as Celtic drew 2–2 with Rangers at Ibrox to win the league in what had been billed as a title decider.

Then there was Lisbon. Jimmy later joked that the look on the faces of the Inter Milan players was a picture as Celtic lined up beside them. The swarthy Italians looked like film stars, while the Celtic players were caked in sunscreen, missing teeth and full of cheek and banter. Looks can be deceiving though and

Celtic, with Johnstone at the top of his game, taught Inter Milan a lesson.

LAST GOAL

Jimmy Johnstone's off-pitch antics were the stuff of legend. Jock Stein once said that his greatest achievement was prolonging Jinky's career, yet Celtic's iconic manager made one of the most difficult decisions of his life when he told Jimmy his career with the club was coming to an end in the summer of 1975. Jinky later said:

> Leaving Celtic broke my heart. I'd been there for fourteen years and it was a like a regular job. Jock spoke to me and said it was time to call it quits, but he gave me a testimonial and that was something to look forward to.

Jimmy's last goal came against Dundee on 14 December 1974, in a 6–0 win. Celtic finished third in the league that season as a run of nine successive titles came to an end. They still won the two cups, but Jimmy only featured in the League Cup triumph over Hibernian, scoring in a 6–3 win. As he departed, his heart remained at Celtic but his playing career would last for another few years. He played for Dundee where he teamed up with a young Gordon Strachan. 'Jimmy was my football hero,' the former Celtic manager said. 'Not everybody knows that we played together at Dundee. It was probably the smallest right-wing combination of all time.'

Jimmy also played for San Jose Earthquakes, Sheffield United, Shelbourne, Elgin City and Blantyre Celtic before calling time on his playing career. He worked as part of David Hay's coaching staff at Celtic before dropping out of the game altogether. In

Celtic's forward line in the 1928 Scottish Cup final, featuring four Century Bhoys. From left to right: Paddy Connolly, Alec Thomson, Jimmy McGrory, Tommy McInally and Adam McLean.

Bobby Lennox lays off the ball to great friend Jimmy Johnstone in a victorious 1973 League Cup sectional game at Ibrox.

Henrik Larsson pulls the trigger on one of the most important goals he scored for Celtic as he puts the club into the 2003 UEFA Cup final at the expense of Boavista.

©SNS GROUP

©PA IMAGES

Two greats for the price of one – Jimmy Quinn looks on while Patsy Gallacher tries another trick from his repertoire against Hearts.

©PA IMAGES

Stevie Chalmers scores the equaliser against Hibernian in the 1961 Scottish Cup quarter-final.

Celtic's 1908 line-up, including Jimmy McMenemy (middle row, fourth from the left) and Jimmy Quinn (front row, fifth from the left).

John 'Yogi' Hughes is denied by the St Mirren defence in a match from 1969.

Sandy McMahon (front row, centre) in a Celtic team photograph from 1897.

©SNS GROUP

Dixie Deans scores against Hibernian in the 1972 Scottish Cup final.

©SNS GROUP

Willie Wallace is challenged by Aberdeen's Martin Buchan during the 1970 Scottish Cup final.

The Greatest Ever Celt – Jimmy 'Jinky' Johnstone.

Charlie Nicholas and Frank McGarvey celebrate Celtic's 1982 League Cup success.

Kenny Dalglish in action against Partick Thistle, challenged by defender Alan Hansen, while Dixie Deans waits to pounce.

Celtic in 1915, with Jimmy McColl (back row, far right).

©SNS GROUP

Harry Hood fires in another goal against Rangers.

©SNS GROUP

Brian McClair heads home against Rangers in the 1986 Ne'erday Derby.

Bobby Collins scores Celtic's third goal against Rangers in a 1957 Scottish Cup tie that finished 4-4.

Johnny Campbell wearing Lord Rosebery's primrose and pink for Scotland.

Neilly Mochan was a fitness fanatic as a player and as a coach.

John Hartson hits a spectacular strike against Liverpool at Anfield in the quarter-final of the UEFA Cup back in 2003.

Joe Cassidy (left) and John Divers Jnr (right).

The peerless Bobby Murdoch in action against Rangers.

retirement, he had his troubles at times, but Jimmy was always a popular figure at Celtic Park and there was shock when it was revealed that he was battling Motor Neurone Disease. In 2002, he was the clear winner of the Greatest Ever Celt award and was voted into the club's Greatest Team, alongside Ronnie Simpson, Danny McGrain, Tommy Gemmell, Bobby Murdoch, Billy McNeill, Bertie Auld, Paul McStay, Kenny Dalglish, Henrik Larsson and Bobby Lennox. It was a fitting tribute.

He was fit enough to attend that ceremony but his health deteriorated in the years that followed and his public appearances became increasingly rare. Yet, throughout his battle, Jimmy fought bravely and worked tirelessly to raise awareness and funds for those who suffered the disease. The world of football then mourned as Jimmy passed away on 13 March 2006. He left behind his beloved wife Agnes and three children.

His funeral was a celebration of the life of a true football great. Tributes poured in from all over the world, while thousands of Celtic supporters and fans of all different clubs lined the streets surrounding Celtic Park as Jimmy Johnstone made his final journey following the funeral mass at St John the Baptist church in Uddingston on 17 March. A few days later, Celtic beat Dunfermline 3–0 in the final of the League Cup. It was dubbed the 'Jimmy Johnstone Final' and as Neil Lennon held aloft the trophy, the wee man would have been proud.

HIGHS AND LOWS

Domestically, Jimmy's career at Celtic was one big fairytale until the day Jock Stein told him that it was time to seek pastures new. While that was a crushing blow at the time, he could later reflect on the best years of his career at Celtic, where he emerged into a new team and helped himself to eighteen major domestic honours, including nine league championships. At times, Jimmy was no angel on or off the pitch, but the highs far outweighed the lows in a domestic sense.

As for Europe, where do you start? Jimmy was a star of the Celtic side who reached the semi-final of the Cup-Winners' Cup in 1963/64 but that was just the warm-up for what was to come next. Despite his huge fear of flying, Jimmy simply revelled in the European arena. His greatest games for Celtic include the 1967 final itself and the 4–0 and 5–1 maulings of St Etienne and Red Star Belgrade in 1968, where he was arguably playing at the peak of his incredible powers. At that stage, he had just turned twenty-four.

The game against Red Star particularly stands out because Johnstone had been told by Jock Stein that he didn't need to travel for the second leg if Celtic won by four clear goals. Jimmy was unplayable and scored twice as Celtic humiliated Red Star. The next day, Jimmy reminded his manager of his promise and eventually got him to keep it. Yet, there was genuine disappointment among the Red Star officials that Johnstone hadn't travelled. 'They couldn't believe he wasn't there, they thought he was in the hamper,' said John Hughes.

Yet, there was better to come. In 1970, Celtic were drawn against Leeds United in the semi-final of the European Cup and Johnstone gave the English side's highly-rated fullback, Terry Cooper, the chasing of his life over two legs. Celtic beat Don Revie's team 3–1 on aggregate and Johnstone was at his irrepressible best.

'Jinky was out of this world at Elland Road,' said teammate Tommy Gemmell.

Cooper must have nightmares every time somebody mentions Jimmy because he gave him a total going over. Norman Hunter shouted 'Kick him' and Cooper turned and shouted back, 'You come out and kick him.' Hunter came out and tried to kick wee Jimmy. Wee Jimmy just waltzed away and nut-megged him.

Yet, while the games against Inter Milan, St Etienne, Red Star Belgrade and Leeds United saw Jimmy scale unbelievable heights, there were setbacks along the way. He was sent off for retaliation after being kicked black and blue by Racing Club in the doomed World Club Championship contest, while losing 2–1 to Feyenoord in the 1970 European Cup final was a disaster for Celtic and Johnstone. He later admitted that Stein's men had taken their opponents lightly: 'We had never really heard about them because Dutch football was just coming to the fore. We underestimated them and that was our own fault.'

In 1971, Jimmy scored his penalty as Celtic were knocked out by Inter Milan in the semi-final of the European Cup in a shoot-out. Three years later, he showed remarkable restraint in the 1974 European Cup semi-final as Atlético Madrid's dirty tactics centred on kicking Jimmy every time he got on the ball. His reputation across Europe, forged in Lisbon and augmented by a series of world-class displays, evidently went before him.

AND ANOTHER THING …

Jimmy Johnstone is the only Celtic player to ever finish in the top three of the Ballon d'Or voting for the European Footballer of the Year award. Unsurprisingly, this accolade was given to him after his wonderful 1966/67 campaign. Manchester United's Bobby Charlton finished second and Florian Albert won the award. No other Celtic player has ever finished in the top three.

One of Jimmy's greatest ever games for Celtic came in a testimonial for Real Madrid legend Alfredo Di Stefano at the Bernabeu in June 1967. Celtic, newly crowned European champions, outclassed the Spanish giants with Jinky setting up Bobby Lennox's goal in a 1–0 win. Jimmy was outstanding that night. By the end, the Real Madrid fans greeted his every touch with 'Olé, olé.' At time up, he lifted the ball to the sky as he was given a standing ovation. Lennox later said: 'He was at the top of his game and Madrid must have tried to sign him after that match, they must have.' We'll never know for sure, but Jimmy was definitely remembered in Madrid. At his funeral in 2006, Di Stefano sent a telegram paying tribute to him.

It remains a crying shame that Johnstone only won twenty-three caps for Scotland. He is widely regarded as one of the best players to be produced by this country but was never classed as a regular, despite being the shining light of the all-conquering Celtic side. He scored four goals in those twenty-three caps but never got the chance to play in the World Cup, despite travelling to Germany in 1974. That was a huge blow, but Jimmy remained pragmatic about it:

> I preferred playing for Celtic. I had a couple of bad experiences playing for Scotland, when I was booed by our own fans. I may not have been playing well, but I didn't feel right after certain fans booed me because I was a Celtic player.

Bertie Auld, his great friend and teammate, believes his cap tally is a disgrace: 'Jimmy should have had 100 caps.'

As well as having football talents, Jimmy was also a talented singer and went into the recording studio on more than one occasion. He produced a version of 'Passing Time' during his playing days and also teamed up with Simple Minds' frontman Jim Kerr for a duet on the Irish folk classic, 'Dirty Old Town', for a Motor Neurone Disease charity single.

Jimmy had a fiery temper on the pitch, mostly brought about

by the rough treatment he would receive on the pitch from defenders. One year after Lisbon, Jock Stein subbed him and Jinky, furious at being brought off, threw his jersey into the dugout. He ran into the dressing room with his manager chasing after him and later admitted: 'I heard Jock's footsteps and almost ran straight out of the stadium and down London Road.'

Jimmy's worldwide influence became evident when he was immortalised in a range of Fabergé eggs celebrating his life and career. A total of nineteen diamond-studded eggs, featuring replicas of his Celtic medals, were created by Sarah Fabergé, the great-granddaughter of Carl Fabergé, the Russian royal court jeweller, who became fascinated with Jimmy's life after watching a documentary about him. Sir Alex Ferguson, Manchester United's manager, was one of the people who bought the special Jimmy Johnstone Fabergé egg.

14

TOMMY McINALLY

128 GOALS IN 213 APPEARANCES

Still only twenty and already some sort of cult hero with the Parkhead faithful as a goalscorer (thirty-six goals in all games) and a fine player with loads of trickery and panache, the personality defects that led to his downfall were not yet apparent. The summer of 1920 was passed by Celtic fans in quiet contemplation of how, with Tommy McInally on board, the team would once again come to dominate Scottish football. Alas, the reality would be somewhat different.

David Potter's excellent biography of the player, *Tommy McInally: Celtic's Bad Bhoy,* recounts the fascinating story of a unique character in Celtic's history. Tommy McInally's life and times occasionally read like an adventure from a *Boys' Own* story, at other times like a script from a Hollywood blockbuster; football's answer to *Raging Bull,* with the dramatic rise and fall of a flawed genius.

That's what Tommy McInally was, and there appears to be a consensus that his talents, God-given as they were, were ultimately squandered.

David Potter writes that:

One of the paradoxes often said about Tommy (and indeed it has been said about George Best, Maradona, Jimmy Johnstone and others) is that 'if he hadn't been such a great player, he could have been even better.' At first, this sounds absurd, but what is meant is that Tommy was such a supremely talented player that he felt that he did not need to bother training or take himself seriously. He was anything but the supremely dedicated professional that we have seen in Kenny Dalglish and Henrik Larsson, as well as in count-less others of lesser ability. Had he only behaved himself, he might have taken Celtic to unbelievable heights of success and prolonged his own career by many more years.

Yet Tommy McInally still managed over 200 appearances for Celtic in two spells at the club – 1919–22 and then 1925–28 – and he did score 128 goals for the club.

His failure to reach his full potential is an accusation that can probably also be levelled at the club during this time, with the 1920s failing to produce the level of success and silverware that the first twenty years of the twentieth century had. Celtic were no longer the dominant team in Scottish football, though still had great players and great entertainers in their ranks. Tommy McInally was most definitely one of them.

FIRST GOAL

There can be no better way to begin a Celtic career than for a player to score on his debut. In fact, that's not strictly true as Tommy McInally proved when he pulled on the green and white Hoops for the first time when Celtic played Clydebank on the opening day of the league season on 16 August 1919. He wasn't content with just the one goal and announced his arrival on the post-First World War football scene with a hat-trick.

It took him all of seven minutes to score the first of his 128 goals for Celtic, and he added two more in the second-half of a match that the Hoops won 3–1. It was a good start to the season for the defending champions but, more importantly, it was a breathtaking start to McInally's Celtic career, prompting the *Glasgow Herald* to declare that, 'The Celts appear to have secured in McInally a worthy successor to Quinn.'

If anyone thought the claim hasty and somewhat bold, then McInally's hat-trick in Celtic's next game just two days later – another 3–1 win, this time against Dumbarton – appeared to provide evidence to the contrary.

He scored the first just before half-time and netted the third in the last minute, though some sources have credited Jimmy McMenemy with providing the final touch to put the ball in the net.

Take a hatful of superlatives, draw any one out and they could apply to Tommy McInally's early Celtic career. After back-to-back hat-tricks, his continued prowess in front of goal in the early stages of the 1919/20 campaign made him an instant hero with the fans. Celtic won their first nine league matches, with the nineteen-year-old McInally netting sixteen goals in those fixtures. This included a third hat-trick, against Clyde on 27 September, while there were doubles against Raith Rovers, Third Lanark and Hibernian.

Despite their excellent start to the season, however, the defending champions relinquished their title, finishing three points behind Rangers who also knocked them out of the Scottish Cup. And it would be another couple of seasons before McInally would gain his first winner's medal, when the Hoops lifted the 1921/22 championship.

The league was clinched at Cappielow on 29 April thanks to a 1–1 draw against Morton, though McInally wasn't in the starting XI, having been out of the first team since the beginning of March.

Within a couple of months of that title triumph, McInally would leave Celtic Park for Third Lanark, his relationship with manager Willie Maley having deteriorated by that point, though they would later try and re-establish a working relationship when McInally returned in 1925. But it remained a difficult one, owing in no small part to McInally's character on and off the park, which left supporters sometimes feeling that he didn't always give every-thing to the cause; an unforgiveable attribute in Maley's eyes.

100TH GOAL

A year after he returned to Celtic following a three-year spell with Third Lanark, Tommy McInally scored his 100th goal for the Hoops. It came on the opening day of the 1926/27 season when the defending champions travelled to Rugby Park to face Kilmarnock. This was before the custom of beginning a new season at home when the league flag could be raised in front a jubilant support.

Kilmarnock were in no mood to acknowledge Celtic's achieve-ments of the previous season and took the lead after just three minutes. McInally provided the equaliser on fourteen minutes, a goal that was also his own personal milestone, and Jimmy McGrory put the team 2–1 ahead before the break. Adam McLean made it 3–1, although the home side pulled a late goal back to reduce the deficit.

McInally's achievement of reaching 100 goals was a worthy one – apparently done in a change strip of green and white quar-ters which Celtic had worn against Kilmarnock on 14 August 1926 – although there remains a feeling of what might have been.

Certainly, the way he began his Celtic career would have suggested that McInally might have reached his century a lot sooner than he did, although it is perhaps an indication of the unique – or flawed – nature of his character that he didn't achieve everything that his prodigious talents had suggested when he'd first broken into the Celtic starting XI.

Still, regardless of what might have been or what could have been, the reality is that he was a superb player and a goal tally of 128 is no mean feat.

Celtic had kicked off season 1926/27 as champions, and with Jimmy McGrory in fine goalscoring form – he would net forty-nine league goals in that campaign – confidence was high that the Hoops could retain their title.

Yet, despite outscoring every other team in the league with a final tally of 101, Celtic still finished third that season, seven points behind Rangers.

McInally was a regular in the side, though he only managed to score eleven goals, including two in the Scottish Cup. That helped Celtic reach the final where they took on East Fife.

Celtic won the final 3–1, though later match reports did highlight the number of chances McInally missed when the Hoops were cruising in the second-half, with some speculating that the forward had done so deliberately.

LAST GOAL

Tommy McInally's final Celtic goal came at the tail-end of the 1927/28 season, which would also prove to be his last with the club. St Johnstone were the visitors to Celtic Park on 18 April 1928, just four days after Celtic had lost 4–0 to Rangers in the Scottish Cup final.

It was a second-half collapse for the Hoops, who conceded all four goals after the break, and it was a stark reflection of the disillusionment of the Celtic support that only 3,000 turned up at Celtic Park for the match after 118,115 had attended Hampden for the final. McInally opened the scoring for the Hoops after twenty-five minutes and Adam McLean doubled the lead five minutes after the interval.

The final goal of the game, which gave Celtic a 3–0 victory, came on the hour mark and it was also McInally's 128th and last goal in Celtic colours.

Once again Jimmy McGrory topped the scoring charts with an impressive 53 goals, while McInally netted 19 for the season. But unfortunately for the player and the club, his final season in the Hoops didn't bring any trophies back to Celtic Park. The team finished runners-up to Rangers in the league, while the Ibrox side beat Celtic 4–0 in the Scottish Cup final.

He left Celtic in May 1928 along with Adam McLean, both players joining Sunderland, the latter, in particular, surprised and reluctant to leave, but perhaps being punished for having made representations to the club about the money being offered for a close-season tour of the United States.

Celtic's legendary parsimony at that time had already raised its head at the 1927 Scottish Cup final, and not for the first time either, but a request by captain Jimmy McStay, no doubt inspired by Tommy McInally, for a win bonus was dismissed by Willie Maley.

HIGHS AND LOWS

There are so many highs and lows to Tommy McInally's life and career, particularly at Celtic, that you could write a book about him. Indeed, that's what author David Potter recently did, and in the book he concludes that:

It is just a shame that Tommy did not always do what he could have for Celtic and their supporters. But then again, if he had always behaved, never smoked or drunk, never argued with authority, never disputed a referee's decision,

never been anything other than a model professional ...
then he would not have been Tommy McInally!

It is unarguable that he was a supremely talented footballer, but it is also undeniable that his talent was not fully exploited. Tommy McInally could, and probably should, have been up there with the greatest-ever Celts. His exploits and his contribution to the club are certainly more impressive than many players', including the fact he scored 128 goals in the green and white Hoops, but supporters at the time were left frustrated, due in no small part to the fact that they could see the ability McInally had and the fact that he seemed to take it for granted and allowed it to fritter away.

Their frustration, however, was not really because of any loss McInally suffered as an individual. It was because they could see that it was Celtic who suffered as a result. That was the most disappointing and, amongst some supporters, the most unforgivable aspect of McInally's tenure at Celtic.

He won just three major trophies with the club: the league championship in 1921/22 during his first spell at Celtic Park; and again in 1925/26 in his first season back after playing for Third Lanark; and the Scottish Cup in 1927 when Celtic defeated East Fife 3–1 in the final.

AND ANOTHER THING ...

Tommy's McInally's older brother, Arthur, was a centre half who played one game for Celtic on 15 December 1917. The Hoops won that match 4–3 though, as David Potter's book explains, that game revealed much about the chaotic nature of football and society at that time during The Great War.

Alec McNair was due to play at right back, but couldn't get a train from Stenhousemuir to Motherwell as transport had been so disrupted. The game was delayed ten minutes, but still no Alec.

It being December, the game had to start to guarantee a finish in daylight. After ten minutes' play, Maley decided to give up on any chance of McNair arriving, moved right half Jimmy Wilson back to right back, then put Arthur McInally, nominally a centre half, into the right-half position. By all accounts, Arthur played well, as Celtic won a tight game 4–3.

There was also an older brother, John, who was also a footballer, playing for Paisley side, Abercorn. But of three McInallys, it was Tommy who was blessed with the greatest talent, achieved the most in the game, but who arguably didn't fulfil the potential that his talents suggested.

15

CHARLIE NICHOLAS

125 GOALS IN 249 APPEARANCES

There is a lineage of individual talent that jinks and weaves its way through the course of Celtic's history, players who possess what would be described in twenty-first century parlance as 'The X-Factor'. Patsy Gallacher had it, as did Charlie Tully, Jimmy Johnstone and Aiden McGeady. There is talk that current Celtic youngster, Islam Feruz could be hewn from the same stone. Charlie Nicholas had it too.

When he burst onto the scene in 1980, a goalscoring teenager whom Celtic had nurtured throughout his formative years, supporters – who were slowly getting used to life without Jock Stein in charge and finally accepting that the Lisbon Lions were part of history and no longer making it before their eyes – acclaimed the youngster as a new hero.

True, Billy McNeill's side already contained players who would become bona fide Celtic legends, such as Danny McGrain and Tommy Burns, and their contribution would far outweigh and outlast their younger colleague, but at the time it was Charlie Nicholas who became the darling of the Celtic fans. So it always was and so it always will be.

Football fans, in the fullness of time, will recognise true greatness, but put a goalscorer into any team, particularly one with an abundance of skill and character, and throw in a dash of youthful impudence for good measure, and it's guaranteed that that will be the name chanted by supporters.

Nicholas had all of these things and in the early 1980s he seemed to embody the flamboyance of the New Romantic era, with carefully styled haircut, trendy clothes – including the requisite absence of socks – and an ability to make the front, as well as the back, pages of the newspapers.

Over and above all that, of course, Charlie Nicholas could play football and did so wonderfully well. He was 'Cheeky Charlie', 'Charles de Goal' and, of course, 'Champagne Charlie'.

He had two spells at Celtic Park. The first, between 1979 and 1983, established his reputation in football and was undoubtedly more productive, successful and probably enjoyable than the five years he spent at the club in the early 1990s.

By then he had spent seven years away from the club. He joined Arsenal where his talents were woefully underused and underappreciated by the management of the club at the time, even if the Arsenal fans took him to their hearts. In 1988, he returned to Scotland though it was not, as many would have expected, back to the East End of Glasgow but to the north-east of the country and Aberdeen, where he helped them lift the Scottish Cup in 1990, scoring one of the penalties in the shoot-out at Hampden to beat Celtic.

By that point he knew he was returning to Paradise but, to his credit, it did not unduly affect or influence his performance in the game or the shoot-out.

Nicholas suffered, as a player and a supporter, when he returned to Celtic. In the middle of what was proving to be a financial maelström, the quality of player diminished and the club drifted inexorably towards its doom, and players such as Nicholas, Paul McStay, Peter Grant and John Collins could not arrest that slide on the park.

He was certainly seen as one of the dressing room agitators

for change at the club, along with other long-standing players, and he welcomed the takeover by Fergus McCann in 1994. Just over a year later, he left the club for a second and final time.

He left behind 125 goals, a lot of wonderful memories, but a lingering sense of disappointment that the status of a true Celtic, and indeed, football great had eluded a player of such outstanding ability.

FIRST GOAL

Charlie Nicholas made his competitive debut for Celtic at Rugby Park, coming on as a substitute for Frank McGarvey who had scored twice in the 3–0 victory over Kilmarnock. The eighteen-year-old was given his first start in the green and white Hoops by Billy McNeill and he came into a squad that appeared to have a good balance of youth and experience in their ranks.

While Danny McGrain was the elder statesman of the group, the likes of Tommy Burns, George McCluskey and Roy Aitken had followed the same career path as Nicholas, progressing through the youth ranks to the first team. McNeill augmented a core of home-grown talent by bringing in the likes of Murdo MacLeod and Davie Provan and it had brought instant success in the shape of the 1979 league title, famously known as the night when 'ten men won the league'.

Having failed to retain the championship, Celtic started season 1980/81 determined to regain the title and while the club harboured high hopes for their teenage striker, they could hardly have expected him to make such an instant and dramatic impact on the club.

Just two weeks after his debut, Nicholas opened his goalscoring account in a game that almost proved to be a disaster for Celtic. Trailing 1–0 to Stirling Albion after the first leg of their League

Cup second round tie, the Hoops made heavy weather of what should have been a routine victory and it took a Tommy Burns goal three minutes from time to level the tie at 2–2 and force extra-time.

It was in that additional half-hour that the full-time side finally showed their superiority and Nicholas, on as a substitute for McCluskey, netted twice. The first of those goals, and the first of 125 that he would score for Celtic, came in the ninety-seventh minute.

He followed that up with eleven minutes of the match remaining as the Hoops won 6–1 to go through 7–2 on aggregate, though the scoreline belied the fact that McNeill's side had struggled.

Nicholas' reward for those two goals was his first start for Celtic in their next game, a home league match against Partick Thistle, and the teenager fired home another two goals in a 4–1 victory.

Celtic had an enviable array of strikers in their ranks at that time, most notably George McCluskey and Frank McGarvey, but it became almost impossible for Billy McNeill to leave Nicholas out of his team. That season, which saw Celtic reclaim the title from Aberdeen, Nicholas made a total of 45 appearances in all competitions, including 39 starts, and he scored an impressive 28 goals, just one less than the club's top goalscorer, McGarvey.

After just one season, it looked as though Celtic had unearthed another diamond while the fans had a new hero to acclaim from the terraces.

100TH GOAL

That it was over eleven years before Charlie Nicholas scored his 100th goal for Celtic tells its own story of his career with the club. In his first three seasons at Parkhead he scored 82 goals, though a closer examination of that total reveals that, in his second season, he only scored 6 goals, missing much of the campaign after breaking his leg in a reserve match at Cappielow in January 1982, while the following year, when he returned to full fitness, he netted an incredible 48 goals in all competitions, including 29 in the league.

Another season in the Hoops and he would have easily and effortlessly reached his century but it was not to be. The bright lights of London came calling in the shape of Arsenal and Nicholas followed a path that had become a well-worn one for Celtic players since the mid 1970s when Lou Macari joined Manchester United.

English football offered financial rewards that Celtic couldn't or wouldn't match and for Nicholas, not yet twenty-two years old, it also provided off-field glitz and glamour that Glasgow's nightlife didn't. Whether Arsenal was the right choice for his prodigious talents remains a point of argument among supporters this day, though the player himself has always said he has no regrets about the move.

His eventual return to Celtic Park in 1990, brought back by the man who'd first given him his chance at the club, did not herald a return to the glory days for Celtic were in the midst of decline that would see them hover on the precipice of annihilation, and the prodigal son could not arrest the fall.

He did, however, reach his century of goals, and it came on 12 October 1991 in a 4–1 victory over Dundee United at Celtic Park in front of what was then a healthy crowd of just over 27,000.

Nicholas scored two that day, the first of which proved to be goal Number 100. Tommy Coyne raced on to a long ball on the right and his low cross was met by Nicholas, who had managed to get ahead of his marker.

He finished the season as the club's top scorer with an impressive 25 goals, though Celtic once again endured a barren campaign, failing to reach either of the domestic cup finals, and finishing third in the league. The team would also lose 5–1 in Switzerland to Neuchatel Xamax, which was the club's heaviest ever European defeat up to that point. The situation at Celtic, however, would get worse before it got better.

LAST GOAL

One of Tommy Burns' first moves after taking over as manager of Celtic from Lou Macari was to re-sign Charlie Nicholas. The player had been released by Macari at the end of the 1993/94 season, but Burns still believed his former teammate could make an important contribution to the cause.

What had appeared to be Nicholas' last season as a Celtic player also proved to be a tumultuous one for the club. Just hours away from going out of business, ex-pat businessman Fergus McCann arrived from Canada at the eleventh hour to save Celtic in March 1994, a move which would herald the steady resurgence of Celtic as a footballing force.

The Hoops finished fourth that season, performing poorly in both cup competitions as well, and Nicholas scored nine goals that season, three less than top goalscorer, Pat McGinlay.

Macari saw the player, now thirty-two years old, as surplus to requirements but unfortunately for the Celtic boss, that was how McCann viewed him and Macari was replaced in the close season by Burns.

Having re-signed for the club, Nicholas would play fifteen times that season, nine as a substitute, scoring just one goal, which would also prove to be his last in the green and white Hoops.

It came at Ibrox on 27 November 1994 in the League Cup final against Raith Rovers, a match that Celtic were strongly expected to win and bring back the first piece of silverware to Paradise since the 1989 Scottish Cup final win over Rangers.

The First Division side took the lead after nineteen minutes through Stevie Crawford but that goal was cancelled out by Andy Walker just after the half-hour mark. And when Nicholas made it 2–1 for Celtic with six minutes of the match remaining, the long-suffering Celtic support prepared to celebrate like it was 1989 … only Raith Rovers hadn't read the script.

A last-minute equaliser from Gordon Dalziel, capitalising on a mistake by Celtic goalkeeper Gordon Marshall, took the game into extra time, and after neither side were able to get a third goal, the match was settled in a penalty shoot-out.

In the cruellest of ironies, it was captain Paul McStay, one of the greatest ever Celtic midfielders and a player who had carried a succession of mediocre Celtic teams through the early 1990s, who missed the vital penalty to give Raith Rovers a 6–5 victory.

They might have been dancing on the streets of Raith, but there was only mourning in the East End of Glasgow and, for Nicholas, it brought to a close his scoring exploits in the Hoops.

HIGHS AND LOWS

Perhaps it should be more of a case of highs, lows and 'what might have been' in the case of Charlie Nicholas. He made 249 appearances for Celtic, scoring an impressive 125 goals, and won league championships in 1981 and 1982, as well as a League Cup in 1982/83, when he scored one of the goals that beat Rangers 2–1 at a rain-soaked Hampden.

Yet, certainly as far as Celtic was concerned, there should be much more to show and so much more to boast of. Nicholas was one of the most exciting talents to burst onto the Scottish game and arguably one of the most naturally gifted players Celtic have ever produced. Indeed, in the early 1980s, it seemed as if the Celtic conveyor belt of talent had been turned back on, with Paul McStay emerging not long after Nicholas.

It wasn't that the striker was obliged to stay at Celtic. The days of the one-club man were becoming increasingly rare – McStay would prove to be one of the last as far as Celtic was concerned – and Nicholas was entitled to seek his fortune elsewhere, as well as challenging himself as a footballer in a different playing environment.

That he chose Arsenal, then managed by George Graham and with a reputation for solid football that relied little on flair and invention, seemed strange to many observers at the time, particularly when it was rumoured that Manchester United and Liverpool were also courting the player.

The gift of hindsight would be the greatest of all, but what if Nicholas has moved to Anfield instead of Highbury, joining one of the best teams in Europe, who had the likes of Dalglish and Souness in their ranks?

During his time at Celtic, particularly during his first spell at the club, Charlie Nicholas was a hero to the support. He might well have earned the moniker 'Champagne Charlie' for his flamboyant lifestyle, though much of that was media invention and, in the early days of the 1980s' excess, turning up to training without wearing any socks marked a player down as a rebel.

He was barely out of his teens, however, when the adulation began to be heaped on his shoulders and who could blame him for enjoying it?

There were moments of personal triumph on the field including the many goals he scored against Rangers, each one becoming in the memory even more spectacular than the one before.

Perhaps his finest goal, and certainly a contender for that title, came against Ajax in Amsterdam on 29 September 1982 in a 2–1 win for Celtic that knocked the Dutch side, Johan Cruyff et al, out of the European Cup. It was the most glorious of chips from the edge of the box, showing technique, audacity and sublime skill that is surely God-given. Only grainy TV footage remains of that moment, but what a moment it was.

AND ANOTHER THING ...

If the newspapers were to be believed, Charlie Nicholas appeared to live up to the nickname 'Champagne Charlie', particularly while he was at Arsenal, and there's no doubt that London was a captivating city for a young Glasgow lad with the world at his skilful feet. Just how much was tabloid invention we may never know, though one apocryphal tale from when he in his first spell at Celtic is certainly entertaining, if not entirely true.

The story goes that the Celtic players were in a Glasgow nightclub one Saturday night when they bumped into a player from another team, who proceeded to declare that he thought Nicholas was an over-rated player, declaring that he could do anything the Celt could.

It was at this point Nicholas produced a £20 note, tore it in half and said: 'Can you do that?' After the player disappeared somewhat sheepishly, it's claimed Nicholas quickly got down on the floor to retrieve the two pieces of the £20.

Whatever the veracity of the story, the truth is, very few players could do what Nicholas was capable of on a football pitch.

Unfortunately, the initial promise and excitement that his first spell at Celtic had created did not flourish in North London. He made 184 appearances for Arsenal, scoring 54 goals and he remains a favourite with Gunners' fans, who saw him as a refreshing alternative to the rigid ordinariness of George Graham's squad.

However, despite signing him, Graham never favoured Nicholas, even after he scored both goals in Arsenal's 2–1 League Cup final victory over Liverpool in 1987.

Nicholas was also capped twenty times for Scotland, scoring five goals, including a wonderful strike on his debut against Switzerland in March 1983.

16

DIXIE DEANS

123 GOALS IN 184 APPEARANCES

The telegram lying on the floor gave very little away. John Kelly Deans picked it up and knew that there was more behind it. For the record, the message read: *'Report to Fir Park at 2.30 p.m. Call Mr Howitt beforehand.'* As Deans, known universally as 'Dixie' in honour of the Everton and England legend Dixie Dean, dialled the digits that would take him through to the office of then Motherwell manager Bobby Howitt, he attempted to guess and second-guess what the nature of the following conversation would be. When he found out, he was left in a state of shock. He was told there and then that Celtic wanted him. That was in October 1971. It remains the best telegram he has ever received and the best phone call he has ever made.

Speaking just weeks after signing for Celtic, Deans was honest enough to admit that the last club he expected to come calling for his services was Celtic. Granted, he boasted a phenomenal scoring record and granted, Lisbon Lions' John Hughes, Stevie Chalmers, Willie Wallace and Joe McBride had now departed. But this was Celtic. This was a side that could call upon Bobby Lennox, Kenny Dalglish, Lou Macari, Harry Hood and George Connelly. They were superstars, every single one of them. 'It just didn't occur that Mr Stein could see me doing a job for him,' was Deans' honest view in his early days as a Celt.

Yet, Jock Stein saw something in Deans that he felt his side lacked. Just like when he plucked McBride from Motherwell, Wallace from Hearts and Hood from Clyde, Stein sensed that Deans would offer something different. Above all, he felt he would provide goals. 'Dixie can do a job in the Joe McBride style and that's all I'm looking for,' was Stein's reasoning. Labelled as one of Scottish football's 'bad boys' when he joined Celtic, Deans knuckled down and started to find the net in prolific fashion. All told, he scored twenty-seven goals as Celtic won the League and Scottish Cup double. His discipline was impeccable.

Domestically, his first season went perfectly, with those 27 goals in 27 games putting him top of the Celtic scoring chart. European football would prove to be a more testing experience. On as a substitute in the second leg of the European Cup semi-final against Inter Milan, he blazed the first penalty over the bar as Celtic lost the shoot-out 5–4. His failure from twelve yards had cost Celtic dearly, yet the supporters never held it against him. Three days later, they gave Deans a standing ovation as he scored twice in a 5–2 win over Motherwell. His hat-trick in the Scottish Cup final win over Hibs that same year assuaged the wounds further. Deans had set a high standard and managed to maintain that form in the following season with thirty-two goals in all competitions as Celtic were again crowned champions. This time, however, the domestic cups proved elusive.

Another league and Scottish Cup double was secured in 1973/74 as Celtic won their historic ninth successive league championship. Deans' goals, all thirty-three of them, were once again pivotal to the club's success. Six of those goals came in the one game against Partick Thistle, when he threatened Jimmy McGrory's proud record of eight goals in ninety minutes. The great man looked on from the stand as Dixie cracked two hat-tricks past Alan Rough in an exceptional performance.

Deans' knack of scoring hat-tricks in cup finals surfaced again in 1974/75 where he hit a treble as Celtic beat Hibernian 6–3 in the League Cup final. Hibs' Joe Harper also scored a hat-trick, which left the two opponents fighting for the match ball.

His Celtic career ended in June 1976. After five years and 184 games, he had 123 goals to his name and had fully justified Stein's unstinting faith in him. In terms of honours, he had pocketed three League titles, two Scottish Cups and one League Cup. He also wore the blue of Scotland twice. After a spell in England with Luton, his career led him to Australia, via Partick Thistle and Carlisle. Now a publican and match-day host at Celtic Park, few players could match Deans' voracious appetite for goals.

FIRST GOAL

Celtic supporters had to wait four long weeks for a glimpse of new signing Dixie Deans. The former Motherwell striker was in the midst of a six-week suspension when he signed for Jock Stein on the last day of October 1971 and was resigned to kicking his heels on the sidelines for the best part of a month.

At that point, Deans' ability was unquestioned but his temperament, which saw him being sent off five times for Motherwell, mostly for dissent, was viewed as suspect. In one of his first interviews as a Celtic player, the man himself stated that he would have to change his ways. 'Apart from playing well, I have to learn to keep my mouth shut,' Deans said. He more than kept his word as Stein's managerial style kept him in check. 'Big Jock terrified me,' he would later reveal. He was sent off only once for Celtic and that was in a reserve game in 1975.

Finally, on 27 November 1971, Deans made his debut in an away match against Partick Thistle and rounded off a 5–1 win with his first goal for the club. It came in the eighty-sixth minute of the match at Firhill and was the start of Deans' crusade to score as many goals as possible against the Jags, as his six strikes in that 1973 contest would suggest. The striker, then aged twenty-five, had joined an unbelievably strong Celtic squad and faced a challenge just to get a game. The Lisbon Lions were still there in force, with Jim Craig, Billy McNeill, Jimmy Johnstone, Bobby Lennox and Bobby Murdoch all regulars in Stein's team.

Added to that, Lou Macari, Davie Hay, Kenny Dalglish and George Connelly, known collectively as the Quality Street Kids, were now an integral part of the squad, while Harry Hood had arrived from Clyde and Tommy Callaghan from Dunfermline.

Yet Deans soon cemented his place in an adventurous Celtic line-up and set about repaying the faith Stein had shown in him with six goals in his first five games for the club. That form ensured he became a fixture in the first team.

Deans' record during his first season as a Celtic player is staggering. Despite only playing from late November onwards, he finished as Celtic's top scorer in the League and Scottish Cup. In total, he scored twenty-seven goals in both competitions.

Along the way, he made his own bit of history as well with a hat-trick in the 6–1 Scottish Cup final win over Hibernian in May 1972. He remains the last Celtic player to have hit a treble in the showpiece game of the Scottish season and he did it in style.

His first was a bullet header from Bobby Murdoch's pinpoint cross. His second was a goal of poise, skill and clinical finishing. Beating the Hibernian goalkeeper Jim Herriot to the ball, he jinked past John Brownlie on the byline, danced infield and then rifled his shot into the rigging. His instinctive forward-roll celebration, perfectly executed, became immortalised in the opening sequences of *Scotsport* in the aftermath of that final. A third goal rounded off an incredible performance.

One major black spot in an otherwise golden season was the missed penalty against Inter Milan in the European Cup semi-final. The fact that Deans was entrusted with the first penalty of the shoot-out said everything about his ability to hit the back of the net. Unfortunately, his aim let him down for once as he scooped his effort over the bar. Even then, there was no accounting for the efficiency of the Inter players, who scored five out of five to take their place in the final.

100TH GOAL

Trust Dixie Deans. He knew he was on the verge of reaching a century of goals for Celtic. He wanted to do it in style. What better way than a cup final hat-trick? Deans' second in the 1974 6–3 League Cup final win over Hibernian at Hampden was his 100th as a Celtic player. It came in 65 minutes and put Celtic 4–2 up. Two minutes later, he hit goal Number 101 to make it 5–2. He shared the match ball with Joe Harper of Hibs – another man who could boast a cup final hat-trick – but Deans was the undoubted star of the show. He was unplayable.

Deans' second goal of the game – his 100th as a Celtic – was a moment of genius. Taking Steve Murray's pass, he let the ball go through his legs before knocking it into space with a deft flick. Shrugging off the attentions of the Hibs defender, he rolled his shot into the corner and took the acclaim of the Celtic support. 'The champagne was opened as soon as we walked into the dressing room,' Deans told *Scotsport's* Arthur Montford after the game. His forward-roll celebration also surfaced again. He thrived on the limelight.

Deans loved scoring against Hibs. He must have done because he did it no fewer than 19 times in 14 games against them in his Celtic career. Pat Stanton and Co. were no soft touches in those days. In Deans, however, they met their match. They must have been glad to see the back of him when he departed. Celtic finished third in the league that season and won the two domestic cups, yet Deans had a frustrating campaign, continually blighted by injury. In total, he made just twenty-six appearances. True to form, he still managed a more than respectable fourteen goals.

His cup final hat-trick also coincided with his elevation to the Scottish national team. A patriotic Scot, those two caps brought him great satisfaction, he faced East Germany in October 1974 and Spain the following month. Bizarrely enough, in terms of goals, 1974/75 would prove to be his worst season as a Celtic player. Yet Deans had nothing to be ashamed of. Years after being brought to the club by Stein, he was still an integral part of the Celtic squad. In the previous season, he had notched a prolific 33 in 44 games, which was his best return as a Celt. Deans' goal had secured Celtic's ninth successive league title.

His assets were varied. He would have been classed as a traditional, chunky striker, the kind who used his bulk to torment defenders. His deceptive pace though, set him apart from forwards of similar stature. At 5ft 8ins, Deans wasn't the tallest, yet could time his leap to perfection and scored an extraordinary amount of goals with his head. In terms of signings, Deans was one of the best Jock Stein ever pulled off. It's to Deans' eternal credit that the loss of Lisbon Lions' Stevie Chalmers, Joe McBride and Willie Wallace wasn't felt as much at it could have been. He had big shoes to fill when he walked through the doors of Celtic Park for the first time, but never shirked a challenge and wrote himself into Celtic folklore by doing what he did best … scoring goals.

LAST GOAL

There was pressure on Dixie Deans as he placed the ball on the spot and stepped back. It wasn't as intense as the glare he had encountered against Inter Milan four years earlier but there was pressure nonetheless. Had he known the enormity of the occasion, perhaps Deans would have felt the strain even more. On the surface, he had to score that penalty to haul Celtic back into a game against Ayr United that they were losing 2–0. He had to try to rescue a Celtic title challenge that had all but faded when Hibernian had inflicted a 2–0 defeat just days earlier.

History also tells us that it was his last, golden chance to score a goal for Celtic. Deans would make one further appearance for Celtic after that Ayr match. Within weeks, he would be on his way to Luton. Deans scored that penalty. Of course he did. Yet the 16,000 supporters inside Celtic Park on 24 April 1976 would never have known they were witnessing Dixie Deans' last goal for Celtic.

Season 1975/76 was strange for all concerned at Celtic. Jock Stein, battling back to health after a serious car crash, had to hand over his managerial duties to Sean Fallon and a rare event occurred; Celtic never won a trophy. The last barren season had been 1963/64. Over the next twelve years, Celtic had lifted trophy after trophy. They had won nine consecutive titles, they been annual visitors to Hampden and they had conquered Europe. Deans had played his part in that dominance.

To his credit, Deans kept scoring to the end. In his final season as a Celtic player, he made thirty-five appearances. His goal tally was seventeen. Only Kenny Dalglish bettered that record in a season of collective decline for the club. It was soon time for Deans to depart from Celtic. A spell with Luton followed, before he surfaced in Australia, playing for Juventus of Adelaide. Down under, the soccer league was still pretty much in its infancy and Deans was an instant hit, with his all-action style making him a fans' favourite. His 30 goals in 57 games didn't harm his cause either as Deans finished his career just like he'd started it ... on the goal trail.

HIGHS AND LOWS

Dixie Deans still has that ball. It looks its age now but it's still in his possession and will remain so forever. After that? Who knows what will become of it, but this priceless piece of Celtic memorabilia won't have any trouble finding a home; just like Dixie didn't have any trouble finding the net on the day he stuck six past Partick Thistle in November 1973.

With hindsight, it was hard to know who was squirming more at Celtic Park that day, Thistle goalkeeper Alan Rough or Celtic legend Jimmy McGrory. Rough, a soon-to-be Scotland internationalist, would have felt physically sick at the thought of Deans single-handedly humiliating him, yet took it all in good spirits.

Years later, Deans told the story of how he stood in the penalty box during that game, by which point he had grabbed five goals. Rough, known for his sense of humour, asked him if he'd scored four or five. Deans waited for the corner to come in, nodded home yet another goal and then shouted to Rough, 'Six.'

McGrory's discomfort was of a different nature. His record haul of eight goals scored against Dunfermline in 1928 was in serious danger, yet the Celtic icon clapped Deans as vociferously as anyone else in the crowd. As a striker, he would have watched the Celtic man's display with great admiration, regardless of personal records. Deans later recalled:

> I had my photo taken with Jimmy in the days afterwards. We both had our match balls signed by the players who took part in each game. I still have the match ball in my possession with the signatures of all my teammates and the great Jock Stein.

Dixie grew accustomed to having his name mentioned in the same breath as Celtic legends. His hat-trick against Hibernian in the 1972 Scottish Cup final drew comparisons with the mighty Jimmy Quinn. The Croy Bhoy had accomplished that same feat in 1904 for Celtic and Deans was now creating his own bit of history.

What made that feat even sweeter for Deans was the timing. The Hampden match came just weeks after his costly penalty miss against Inter Milan in the European Cup semi-final. It was an understandable low point for Deans, especially as Celtic folklore tells you he had scored every practice penalty he attempted at Seamill, in the run-up to the game. His touch deserted him under the floodlights at Celtic Park, yet the Hoops fans forgave him for that indiscretion.

Scoring a hat-trick in my first Scottish Cup final was a boyhood dream come true. It came just weeks after I'd missed the penalty in the European Cup semi-final against Inter and I'd wondered how the fans would react to me. But they were fantastic that day, so the Scottish Cup final was my payback to them. That was my thank you.

A second Hampden hat-trick against Hibernian, this time in the 1974 League Cup final, ranks as a real highlight of Deans' Celtic career. As he cavorted with his teammates at the national stadium that day, the travails of two years previously must have seemed a million miles away. Tarred as a trouble-maker with a real disciplinary problem, Deans' frustration was compounded by Motherwell's reluctance to let him leave for a bigger challenge. He seriously considered quitting the game he loved until Jock Stein intervened and gave him a chance he couldn't refuse. The rest is Celtic history.

AND ANOTHER THING ...

Dixie Deans was a boyhood Rangers supporter. Or was he? Don't believe everything you read, because the man himself stated years later that this was a common misconception. 'That's something that I'd like to set straight,' he laughed. 'I was never a Rangers supporter. I was a St Mirren supporter and would go to most of their home games. I'd never been to Ibrox in my life until I played against them with Motherwell.'

Regardless of the mystery surrounding his apparent childhood allegiances, Celtic supporters hit it off with Deans from the start. Chants of 'Dixie, Dixie' would rise up into the air as another goal hit the back of the net. Dixie gave his all for Celtic and the supporters appreciated it. Once he even sacrificed his two front teeth for the club in a game against St Johnstone in 1976. He never got them back, as his false dentures prove. Deans said: 'I remember Neilly Mochan came out on to the park and said to me, "They've done a good job, Dixie. They're clean out!" I never did find them.'

He was the last Celtic player to score in a game played on Christmas Day. That was in 1971 and he hit the third in a 3–2 win over Hearts on 25 December. 'Rest assured, it was a cheery Christmas Day at Celtic Park,' said Deans, who also revealed that tee-total boss Jock Stein had presented every member of the Celtic squad with a bottle to celebrate the festive period. Deans played with some iconic figures at Celtic but insists, 'George Best was my favourite player and always has been. Out of all the great players, even taking into consideration the Maradonas and the Peles, George was still the best.'

17

JIMMY McCOLL

123 GOALS IN 169 APPEARANCES

Jimmy McColl was born on 14 December 1892, just three days before Celtic thrashed the 5th Kirkcudbright Rifle Volunteers 7–0 in a Scottish Cup second-round tie, with Johnny Madden scoring five of the goals. It was a season that would see Celtic win their very first league championship though, even when they did clinch it in May 1893, the young baby McColl would have been oblivious to the success of the fledgling East End of Glasgow football club.

As he grew up, he began to show real promise as a footballer and in September 1912, he signed from St Anthony's, a junior team who had preceded Celtic in wearing the green and white Hoops, a month after he'd played a trial game for Celtic.

After dominating Scottish football with six consecutive league titles between 1905 and 1910, Celtic had endured three seasons without a title, although they did manage to win two Scottish Cups with victories in 1911 and 1912. However, Willie Maley wanted to restore what he would have seen as the natural order of things in Scottish football, which was Celtic as champions.

And in McColl's first season at the club, the Hoops duly reclaimed their league crown, finishing the season six points clear of second-placed Rangers, with McColl contributing seven league goals, along with six in the Scottish Cup as Celtic clinched the third league and cup double in their short history. It would be another forty years, however, before they would repeat the feat in season 1953/54.

It was the first of four league titles in a row and McColl would spearhead the attack throughout that period, topping the scoring charts in each of the three following seasons.

He earned the nickname 'Sniper' for his deadly accuracy in front of goal and that's borne out by his record of 123 goals in 169 appearances, an impressive return. He could have scored many more goals for Celtic had the club not opted to sell him in 1920. The evidence to back that up is the 128 goals he scored subsequently for Hibernian after he joined the Edinburgh club in 1922.

FIRST GOAL

If Celtic and their support had been searching for a worthy successor to Jimmy Quinn, who was reaching the end of a remarkable career with the club, then the emergence of Jimmy McColl appeared to suggest that the club has unearthed another goalscoring diamond.

McColl first appeared in the first team on 18 October 1913 in a 1–0 victory over Dundee at Celtic Park when Andy McAtee scored the only goal of the game with eight minutes remaining. He also missed a penalty in that match.

The new Bhoy did enough to keep his place for the next league match – a 2–0 victory against Rangers at Ibrox – and made his third consecutive start on 1 November against Kilmarnock at Celtic Park. Patsy Gallacher gave the home side the lead just before half-time, but it was after the break that Celtic drove home their advantage and scored three further goals without reply, which included Jimmy McColl's first ever goal for the Hoops. Just for good measure, he added a second ten minutes from time to get his tally up and running.

However, it would be another three months before he scored again, having been in and out of the side during that period, though as the season reached a climax, both in the league and Scottish Cup, the name of 'Jimmy McColl' became an increasingly common presence on the team sheet.

After the unprecedented success of the six-in-a-row era between 1905 and 1910, Celtic had gone three years without winning the league, but season 1913/14 saw the championship return to Paradise as the Hoops finished six points clear of Rangers. Just for good measure, Celtic also clinched the third 'Double' in the club's history with an emphatic 4–1 victory over Hibernian in the replay of the final, which was played at Ibrox.

The first match had finished goalless, with Hibs almost snatching victory near the end of the game and for the replay, the wonderfully named Ebenezer Owers was dropped in favour of McColl. It was an inspired move by Willie Maley, with McColl scoring twice inside the first ten minutes to put Celtic in the driving seat. John Browning added two more to bring the Scottish Cup back to the East End of Glasgow, though it would be another forty years before the club won another Double.

For Jimmy McColl, it had proved to be a successful debut season for the club. He scored thirteen goals, his tally second only to the great Patsy Gallacher, while he had two winner's medals to show from his contribution, and they would be followed by a further three league medals as Celtic reasserted their dominance of the Scottish game, inspired by the genius of Gallacher, but helped in no small part by the goals of McColl, who would finish as the club's top scorer in the next three seasons.

100TH GOAL

Having won four league titles in a row, Celtic were beginning to close in on their world record of six as season 1917/18 kicked off, and a 4–0 victory on the opening day of the season against Ayr United was an impressive way to begin another defence of the title.

Jimmy McColl and John Browning both scored twice in that game, with three of the goals coming in an explosive five-minute spell at the start of the second-half, and it was an encouraging sign to the Celtic support that McColl, their top scorer in the triumphs just past, was starting where'd left off the previous season, when he'd signed off with a double in the final game of the campaign against Clyde.

It would again be Celtic's near neighbours who would provide the opposition when McColl netted his 100th goal for the Hoops, and it was part of an impressive hat-trick in a 3–2 victory. Celtic won their first six league fixtures, scoring fifteen goals and conceding just four. McColl contributed eight of those goals, including his milestone 100th, and optimism was high at Celtic Park. Not even a 3–2 home defeat against Kilmarnock, who had been the only team to beat Celtic the previous season, was too concerning at the time, given that in their next match the Hoops beat Rangers 2–1 at Ibrox, with McColl scoring Celtic's equaliser four minutes after the home side had taken a fifteenth-minute lead. Andy McAtee scored the winner nine minutes from time.

Celtic ultimately finished second in the league, a point behind Rangers, when a two-goal home victory against Motherwell on the final day of the season would have made it five-in-a-row for the Hoops. In the event, they could only draw 1–1 despite taking an early lead through Patsy Gallacher.

Crucially, the team had to do without the services of Jimmy

McColl for a large chunk of the season – he didn't play between 10 November 1917 and 2 March the following year – and while Celtic didn't lose any games in that period, they drew five matches including three that finished goalless, and McColl's presence, and goalscoring ability, may well have won at least one of those games, which would have made all the difference come the end of the season.

It's interesting to note that the following season, with McColl a regular in the side once more and scoring, it was Celtic who finished first in the league, a point ahead of Rangers.

LAST GOAL

Celtic won their last six league fixtures of 1918/19 to regain the title and Jimmy McColl scored six goals in those games, including a double against Hearts in the second-last match of the season. It helped the Hoops to a 3–2 victory and meant that the team went into the final game, an away match against Ayr United, knowing that a win would see them crowned champions.

The two goals McColl scored against Hearts brought his tally for the club to an impressive 123, and that would be his final total for the Hoops. He played eight games the following season but didn't manage to find the net, his last game coming against Dundee on 31 January 1920 in a 2–1 defeat at Dens Park.

It was McColl's 169th appearance for the club, and it also high-lighted his impressive goalscoring contribution, with 123 goals in those matches.

Unfortunately, injuries would feature throughout McColl's career but, when fit, there were few better finishers in the game and it did seem as though, with Jimmy Quinn's retirement in 1915, that Celtic had their natural goalscoring finisher.

It seems strange therefore, to look back and see that Celtic let McColl leave just five years later. He joined Stoke City in May 1920 at the age of just twenty-seven, and there's no doubt he still had much more to contribute to football. He would do just that, but it would be in the green and white of Hibernian rather than Celtic that he proved his continuing worth as a player.

HIGHS AND LOWS

Jimmy McColl helped Celtic win five league championships and one Scottish Cup in 1914. There would probably have been more triumphs in the latter competition had it not been suspended during the First World War.

His performance in that cup final, however, when he recovered from injury to lead the line in the replay against Hibernian, proved beyond doubt that Celtic had a player of immeasurable quality.

Jimmy Quinn's career, by this point, was effectively over because of injury, and a patched-up Celtic side did well to hold Hibs to a goalless draw in the first match. McColl made himself available for the replay and duly scored two goals as Celtic won the match 4–1 to lift the famous old trophy for the ninth time, securing a league and cup double in the process.

The league title that season would kick of a four-in-a-row sequence that re-asserted Celtic's dominance in Scottish football and McColl was an integral component in that success, finishing top scorer in the three subsequent seasons, including one year when he scored thirty-four league goals.

There were very few low points during his playing career at Celtic Park, though losing the league title, in 1918, by a point to

Rangers would have grated. They would regain the title the following season.

Undoubtedly the greatest disappointment for Jimmy McColl would have been the fact he was released by Celtic. He joined Stoke City but lasted just over a year in England – apparently his wife didn't settle – before returning to Scotland, joining Partick Thistle, where he stayed a further year until Hibernian came calling.

AND ANOTHER THING ...

Having managed to score 123 goals in the green and white Hoops of Celtic, Jimmy McColl duly went on and scored 128 goals in the green and white of Hibernian, becoming the first player to hit a century of goals for the Edinburgh club. It was an incredible achievement and one that marks him out as one of Scotland's greatest ever goalscorers, with 251 goals to his name.

Despite his phenomenal contribution in terms of goals, Hibernian didn't manage to win a trophy. They twice lost the Scottish Cup final, once to Celtic in 1923, when Joe Cassidy scored the only goal of the game at Hampden in front of an impressive crowd of 82,000.

Amazingly, McColl never won a cap for Scotland, though he does form part of an all-too-large band of Celts who were woefully underappreciated by their country

He later joined Leith and had a brief spell in charge of Belfast Celtic before returning to Easter Road in 1937 where he became trainer. And in 1971, at a public ceremony at the stadium, Hibs recognised Jimmy McColl's contribution to the club by presenting him with a gold watch. He passed away in 1978 at the age of eighty-five, a truly great goalscorer but perhaps not recognised as such by Scottish football, given that his exploits came in the pre-war, pre-television era.

Nevertheless, the statistics speak for themselves and acknowledge Jimmy McColl as a great player in the green and white of east and west.

18

HARRY HOOD

123 GOALS IN 310 APPEARANCES

For years, Celtic and Harry Hood had been avoiding each other. Cupid had been playing funny games, but the marriage that had long proved elusive was finally arranged in 1969. In truth, it was a match made in Heaven.

But for a few twists of fate, Hood should have been a Celtic player long before he was able to pull on the Hoops. He signed for Clyde in 1964 on the night before Sean Fallon was expected to watch him play and decide on his suitability for Celtic. Who knows what would have happened had he delayed his decision by a matter of hours.

Hood came even closer to joining Celtic in November of that year. Clyde were happy with the fee Celtic offered but the personal terms were unacceptable for the player. Hood did leave Shawfield but it was for Sunderland, and not Celtic, that he signed. Once again, Hood had slipped through Celtic's fingers, through no fault of his own.

The striker eventually returned to Clyde and Jock Stein made his intentions clear in 1969. Hood needed little convincing and agreed to join one of the best teams in Europe. Celtic were blessed with exceptional, world-class strikers, but Hood offered something different from the rest. He had skill, poise and a touch of real class. When given a chance in front of goal, he rarely panicked. The supporters loved him and were happy to immortalise another hero in a varied repertoire of songs.

Hood's 123 goals in 310 appearances prove that his signing was another masterstroke from Stein. He augmented a vibrant group of forwards and the medals flowed. He won the League Cup in 1969 to pick up his first piece of silverware and never looked back. When Harry left Celtic in 1976, he took away five Scottish League medals, three Scottish Cup medals and two League Cup medals. That was not a bad haul all told. He won the league every season from 1969/70 to 1973/74 and lifted the Scottish Cup in 1971, 1974 and 1975 and the League Cup in 1969 and 1974. In 1970/71, Hood was Celtic's top scorer with 33 goals.

In a fiercely competitive era, full international honours never came Harry's way, but his club exploits made up for that disappointment. Aside from Celtic, he also played for Clyde, Sunderland, Motherwell and Queen of the South. He also had a spell in America after leaving Celtic. Wherever he went, Hood scored goals. That knack never deserted him.

Hood deserves his place in Celtic folklore. He wasn't a Lisbon Lion or a Quality Street Kid, but he fitted in perfectly at Celtic. He had the X-Factor that helped the team win games and in many ways he was the classic Celtic player. His record of 123 goals and ten major honours stands comparison with the greats.

FIRST GOAL

In the 1960s, there were no transfer windows and the football world was a better place. It meant clubs could sign players when they wanted and Jock Stein used this freedom of movement to his advantage when he brought Harry Hood to Celtic on 16 March 1969. The Celtic manager clearly felt that Hood's class and eye for a goal could prove crucial in the run-in.

As always, Stein was right. Less than two weeks after signing for Celtic, Hood made his debut and scored his first competitive goal for the club in a comfortable 3–0 away win over St Mirren on 29 March. Hood, who wore the No.8 shirt for Celtic, had scored for the reserves against Hibernian three days earlier and impressed enough to win a place in the side. Stein praised his 'intelligent, clever play' in both games.

His instant impact meant that Hood was soon thrust into the first team on a weekly basis and he repaid his new manager's faith by scoring the winning goal in a 3–2 win over St Johnstone that virtually sealed the title for Celtic. 'Harry showed he's a first-class buy,' said Stein, talking after the game in Perth.

He finished that season with five goals from just seven appearances for Celtic. Stein hoped he'd make an impression to help Celtic over the finishing line, but it was more immediate than anyone had expected. The Celtic supporters took to Hood and admired his deft touch and scoring prowess. Celtic finished the 1968/69 season as treble winners in Scotland. They had seen off all comers and Hood, while a late arrival, had played his part. He said:

> I had a good start scoring-wise, but I don't think I played particularly well. I went from part-time football at Clyde to full-time with Celtic. It wasn't easy. I was a Celtic fan and maybe the fact I was playing with my heroes was a bit overpowering at first. The training was much more intense as well, but I did settle down eventually.
>
> It was always an ambition of mine to play for Celtic and I was proud to achieve that. All the players were brilliant with me and there was a real camaraderie in the squad. It was great to play my part in such a successful era and an honour to work with Mr Stein. He was a genius. He always kept you on your toes.

100TH GOAL

It was a belated Christmas present for Harry Hood, but remains one of the best he has ever received. 29 December 1973 was the day he joined the elite band of players to score a century of goals for the club. The milestone came in a day of braces for Celtic as Hood, Kenny Dalglish and Dixie Deans all hit doubles in a 6–0 win over Dunfermline at Celtic Park.

Hood's first, which came in the sixty-third minute, was his 100th for the club. It arrived in the midst of another double-winning season for Celtic and was a fitting achievement for Hood, whose consistent scoring record was a pivotal factor in Celtic's dominance of Scottish football in the 1960s and 1970s.

The striker scored eighteen goals for Celtic that term, the third-best tally of his eight seasons at Celtic, and provided grace and guile in the Hoops' frontline. With Deans, Dalglish and Bobby Lennox providing a potent threat, Hood was often asked to link the play and operate in a withdrawn role. Yet, his scoring ratio remained impressive. He recalled:

I scored 123 goals for Celtic, but I didn't always play as a striker. When Kenny arrived on the scene, I dropped a bit deeper. I could pass the ball and play in midfield, so Mr Stein put me in there because there wasn't as much talent in that area of the squad. I often wonder how many I would have scored had I played up front more. To be honest, I hated playing in midfield. I wanted to be a striker.

Hood scored the opening goal as Celtic beat Dundee United 3–0 in the 1974 Scottish Cup final at Hampden. Celtic were 2–0 up within twenty-four minutes that day as they cruised to victory, but there would be no such calm on the European stage. The antics of Atlético Madrid put paid to that.

Even today, Hood winces as he recalls the dirty tricks of the Spanish side. He played in both legs of the European Cup semi-final as Madrid kicked their way to the final. Three Atlético players were sent off in the goalless first leg and Madrid finished the job in Spain.

'That was a low point,' said Hood.

Losing the second leg was hard to take. I had one of my best games for Celtic that day, but a few of the boys were intimidated and rightly so. They threatened to shoot Jimmy Johnstone. From a team point of view, losing that tie was disappointing. I was on the bench for the 1970 European Cup final, but the dirty tactics of Atlético left a bad taste in the mouth. Overall, I think every player from that era regrets that we didn't have more success in Europe.

LAST GOAL

The curtain came down on Harry Hood's Celtic career on 29 April 1976. The striker had spent seven wonderful years at Celtic, but it was time to move on. He moved to America to join San Antonio Thunder and start a new chapter in his life as the Celtic supporters thanked him for his endeavours.

Season 1975/76 was one to forget for Celtic. After dominating Scottish football for the previous decade, Celtic, with Jock Stein absent after a car crash, ended the season with no silverware to their name. Rangers won the Scottish League by six points, while the domestic cups offered no solace. Motherwell defeated Celtic in the third round of the Scottish Cup and Rangers edged a derby League Cup final 1–0. Hood started that match, before being replaced by Jackie McNamara Snr.

Hood made eighteen starts for Celtic that season and scored five goals. One of those goals came in the league against Hearts on 4 October 1975. Celtic won 3–1 that day and Hood opened the scoring. It would prove to be his last in Celtic colours. He said:

> That was a really disappointing season for me. Sean Fallon was in charge that year while Mr Stein recovered from his car crash and I hardly kicked a ball. He wouldn't even let me play in the reserves, but then he'd put me into a big European tie. It was a frustrating year, so I asked for a free transfer and got it.

The club was going through a period of transition and Hood felt that his time was up. He had the option to stay, but didn't feel his situation would improve if Fallon stayed in charge. Therefore, he decided to move on. In hindsight, he could have prolonged his Celtic career.

'If I'd known Jock would definitely be coming back, I'd have probably stayed,' he said.

> I just felt I was the man who missed out under Sean. He's a lovely man but we didn't always agree on football. I felt it was better that I left, so I did.
>
> When I look back on my time at Celtic, I only have good memories apart from the last year. I loved training and playing football. To sit on the bench every week was soul-destroying for me, but that last season doesn't spoil all the good times I had.

HIGHS AND LOWS

Ask someone to name the last Celtic player to score a hat-trick against Rangers and all manner of Hoops strikers will get thrown at you. Henrik Larsson, Kenny Dalglish, Brian McClair, Dixie Deans … they will all get a mention. Harry Hood loves the fact he's the answer to a trivia question.

Regulars at Hood's hotel in Uddingston, have heard the stories a million times by now, but the ex-Celt never gets tired of regaling them with his past achievements. 5 December 1973 was undoubtedly his finest hour in a Celtic strip. It was the night he became 'Hat-trick Harry'.

'It's not every day you score three goals against Rangers. It was fantastic,' said Hood, speaking in the *Celtic View* of 12 December 1973. 'However, the hat-trick wasn't too important. Beating Rangers and qualifying for the League Cup final was the most important thing.'

Close to forty years later, has Hood changed his tune somewhat? If the hat-trick wasn't that important, we should assume he probably hasn't found himself talking about that famous night very often.

'I've had a lot of fun over that hat-trick,' says Hood.

People always talk about it and the question is asked in pub quizzes all across the country. Nobody gives me as the answer either. They go through every Celtic striker of the last forty years, but few people know that it was me who scored the hat-trick.

And it could have been more. Hood slotted home a fourth goal of the evening late on but the effort was disallowed. The referee obviously decided Rangers had been humiliated enough, but Hood still feels a sense of frustration over the one that got away. 'I never realised that nobody had ever scored four goals for Celtic against Rangers in one of the big three competitions,' he said. 'To do that would have been special, but the referee obviously decided not to make a contentious decision.'

Hood had a habit of scoring in important games and his winner against Rangers in September 1969 gave Celtic a first victory at Ibrox for twelve years. It was also Jock Stein's first win there as Celtic manager. In 1970/71, Harry's best as a striker, he also scored the goal against Aberdeen that virtually clinched the title for Celtic. 'I don't know why, but I just had a knack of scoring in big games,' said Hood.

Lows were the European Cup defeats to Feyenoord and Atlético Madrid. He also missed the Inter Milan semi-final in 1972 through injury. Harry's talents should have led to international honours but an Under-23 cap was all he had to show for his efforts, although he did feature on an unofficial Scotland tour in 1967.

AND ANOTHER THING ...

Celtic supporters who frequented Paradise in the Harry Hood era fondly remember the different songs that were used to honour him. One was sung to the tune of 'Robin Hood' while George Harrison's 'My Sweet Lord' was re-jigged in honour of Hood. Some fans also changed the words to the song, 'Hare Krishna'. There was another tune that told how the Celtic supporters rated Hood way above the talents of Eusebio. If Hood was on the bench, the supporters would often chant one of his songs when they felt it was time to introduce him.

Hood played alongside all the Celtic striking greats of that era; Dalglish, Lennon, Johnstone, Chalmers and Deans, to name just a few. Yet the man who stood out for Hood was Willie Wallace. 'I was lucky to play with a lot of great players in my time at Celtic – Kenny, Jimmy and Bobby, the list goes on – but my favourite teammate was Willie Wallace.' said Hood. 'Willie was a great professional and when I was young and just in the team. He taught me a lot.'

Harry's season-by-season record reads as follows: 1968/69 (5 goals), 69/70 (17), 70/71 (33), 71/72 (19), 72/73 (16), 73/74 (18), 74/75 (10) and 75/76 (5).

19

BRIAN McCLAIR

122 GOALS IN 199 APPEARANCES

A training drill on finishing is taking place at Manchester United's Carrington Training Ground and a lone figure is watching closely and barking encouragement at some of the club's youth players. The youngsters are listening intently to his every word and no wonder. Brian McClair is one man who knew the way to goal. It comes as no surprise to those who played with McClair or encountered him, even briefly, that he has gone on to enjoy such success in the coaching side of the game. The Scot, nicknamed 'Choccy', was always a cerebral presence in football as he enjoyed a prolific career.

It's only natural Sir Alex Ferguson, a man who holds McClair in the highest regard, should entrust him with the job of moulding the next generation of United stars. Currently Academy Director with the English giants, McClair is revered at Old Trafford for his exploits during his eleven years as a player with Manchester United. Yet, Celtic will always retain a special place in his heart and he made a considerable impact during a prolific four-year spell at the club.

McClair was nineteen when he was lured to Celtic Park from Motherwell in 1983. He followed a well-worn path of young strikers who moved to Celtic from Fir Park. Before him, Joe McBride and Dixie Deans joined Celtic from Motherwell. Andy Walker and Scott McDonald would later make the same journey.

Not that McClair was your conventional footballer. He had embarked on a Glasgow University course in Computer Maths and combined his studies with his early career as a professional footballer at Motherwell.

Aston Villa was the first club of a player coveted by all the major British clubs at a young age, but that move didn't work out. Instead, Motherwell gave McClair the first-team platform to show off his talents and he exploited that opportunity to the full. The best way for any young striker to catch the attention of bigger clubs is by scoring against them and that was McClair's forte. He grabbed a hat-trick against Rangers and a double against Celtic in two famous Motherwell wins in 1982/83. His departure to a major Scottish football power was only a matter of time after that.

At Celtic, McClair didn't have the best of careers in terms of silverware and there were also spells out of the team, which almost forced him to leave in 1985. Over four years, he was battling with top-class strikers for a regular place and, at one stage, was forced to play a deeper, attacking midfield role that would become his trademark at Manchester United. He delivered goals though. In each of his four seasons at Celtic, he finished top of the scoring charts for his club. His first season yielded 31 goals and he followed that up with 24 in 1984/85. He scored 26 the following season and finished up with an astonishing 41 strikes in his last campaign in the Hoops.

Celtic finished that campaign empty-handed, which also happened in McClair's first season. For someone so prolific, it must be a huge disappointment that he finished his career at Celtic with only two medals in his collection; the 1985 Scottish Cup and 1986 Scottish Premier League title. By 1987, McClair was one of the best strikers in Britain. That was the same year he called time on his Celtic career, leaving to join Manchester United in the summer. The clubs were locked in a dispute over his value, which a tribunal eventually set at £850,000. Even twenty-two years ago, United got an absolute bargain.

McClair wrote himself into Manchester United folklore over the next eleven years. The Scotland internationalist was a central figure in Sir Alex Ferguson's long-term plan but even he couldn't have envisaged the impact McClair would have. He won four Premiership titles, three FA Cups and one League Cup. He scored in both domestic finals and was in the United side that lifted the Cup-Winners' Cup in 1991. He might never have possessed the extravagance of Ryan Giggs or Eric Cantona, but had the guile and experience that was such a hallmark of that great United side. McClair called time on his United career in 1998 and had a brief spell with Motherwell before moving into coaching circles with Blackburn Rovers. He has been United's Academy Director since 2006.

FIRST GOAL

What did Billy McNeill see in Brian McClair when he paid the £75,000 it took to bring him from Motherwell to Celtic in June 1983? Well, the nineteen-year-old had made a real name for himself by scoring goals against the two big Glasgow clubs for the Fir Park outfit, so Cesar felt he was buying a raw, scoring talent that would perfectly augment his blossoming Celtic team. However, by the time McClair made his debut, McNeill had departed and Davie Hay was the new Celtic manager. Naturally, this wasn't an ideal situation for McClair. McNeill was the man who had signed him and now McClair would never get the chance to play under him. However, Hay, who inherited a Celtic squad shorn of two strikers when Charlie Nicholas departed for Arsenal and George McCluskey signed for Leeds United, was the beneficiary of a shrewd piece of business from his predecessor.

Initially, McClair wasn't a regular. He was still classed as a young player, one for the future, and more senior strikers were in front of him. Hay chose the experienced partnership of Jim Melrose and Frank McGarvey to begin with. However, McClair couldn't be kept out of the team for long. His maiden Celtic strike came in a wonderful individual performance against Dundee when McClair struck four times in a 6–2 rout.

His first came in thirty-eight minutes when he pounced on a loose ball and found the bottom corner. He then added a hat-trick in the second period, profiting from Paul McStay and Tommy Burns assists to produce a clinical display. That victory maintained Celtic's 100 per cent start to the season. With five wins out of five, Celtic were in a commanding position, but a run of two draws and two defeats in the next four games would prove damaging for Celtic come the end of the season.

McClair kept scoring and forced Hay to play him. He bagged a string of doubles and hit a hat-trick against his former club Motherwell, but Aberdeen and Dundee United were mounting a strong title challenge and Celtic eventually came up short, finishing runners-up as the Dons took the league title by seven points. Indeed, it was a year of second prizes for Celtic. They lost in the finals of the both the Scottish Cup and League Cup against Aberdeen and Rangers. McClair scored in the latter, a 3–2 defeat.

100TH GOAL

'CHOCCY CHALKS UP A TON' proclaimed the front page of the *Celtic View*, dated Wednesday, 17 December 1986. If the headline isn't self-explanatory, it celebrated Brian McClair's 100th goal for Celtic in all competitions. Fittingly, given his association with Motherwell, the strike came at Fir Park. Interestingly, McClair lined up in midfield for Celtic that day as Alan McInally and Maurice Johnston started up front. It had no impact on McClair's eye for a goal, however. When the 100th strike arrived, it was no surprise that Paul McStay was at the heart of it. He combined with McInally and slid a cross into the box for McClair to finish off a wonderful move.

The fact he finished as Celtic's top scorer in every season he spent at the club illustrates the consistency of McClair, but 1986/87 saw him at his scoring peak. Whether in attack or midfield, he was unstoppable. He scored opportunist goals and spectacular goals and was equally deadly on the ground as in the air. Allied to his football brain, this made for a potent mix. He finished that campaign with 51 goals, 35 of which came in the league. That was a post-war record for Celtic. It is now shared with Henrik Larsson, who claimed the same amount of league goals in 2000/01.

Yet, while Larsson celebrated a treble that season as Celtic managed a clean sweep of trophies, McClair had nothing to show for his efforts. Will a Celtic player ever again score thirty-five league goals in a season and not have a winner's medal to show off at the end of it? Probably not. But that was the reality for McClair as Celtic finished second in the league behind Rangers and lost 2–1 in the final of the League Cup. McClair at least scored a spectacular goal that day as he maintained his habit of finding the net in cup finals.

LAST GOAL

In hindsight, there was a certain irony in the timing of Brian McClair's last Celtic goal. It came just prior to Billy McNeill's return as manager and meant that Cesar, who signed the player in 1983 before his departure, still didn't get the chance to work with him. They were like ships passing in the night. As it turned out, McClair's final goal for Celtic was a penalty against Falkirk in a 2–1 loss on 2 May 1987. By then, the league was over and a crowd of just over 14,000 witnessed the game at Celtic Park.

There would be one final outing in the Hoops for McClair, against Hearts at Tynecastle, but the end was nigh. Sir Alex Ferguson wanted his goals at Old Trafford and McClair – who had been crowned Scotland's Player of the Year – felt United's offer was too good to turn down. It was a decision that changed his life and helped alter the course of United's history as Ferguson's Old Trafford dynasty clicked into gear.

McClair, as expected, was a success at United. He scored over twenty league goals in his first season and in doing so became the first United player since George Best to achieve that feat. That would only be the beginning of a long association with United, but Celtic, in the short-term anyway, didn't suffer from McClair's exit. He was joined in the departure lounge by Maurice Johnston (Nantes) and Alan McInally (Aston Villa). Incoming manager McNeill's striking options had been decimated, but he kept calm and rebuilt his strike force.

Just like McClair had done four years earlier, Andy Walker arrived from Motherwell to team up with Mark McGhee, who was already there. A few months into the season, Frank McAvennie and Joe Miller signed to bolster Celtic's attacking options. Celtic never looked back as they won a double in the club's centenary season, with McAvennie and Walker scoring over fifty goals between them. McNeill, though, must still view McClair as the one who got away.

HIGHS AND LOWS

There is an obvious low in the Celtic career of Brian McClair in that the club competed for 16 trophies during his four years –

12 domestic and 4 European – and won only two of them. Given that he started the 1985 Scottish Cup final on the bench, despite being the club's top scorer, that triumphant day at Hampden could have been more memorable, although he did play a lead role in Celtic's dramatic victory when coming on as a substitute. Davie Provan's free kick brought Celtic level against Dundee United, before Frank McGarvey's instinctive header won it for the Hoops.

McClair's European career with Celtic also featured many highs and lows. He scored as Celtic beat Sporting Lisbon 5–0 at Celtic Park to overturn a 2–0 first-leg defeat in the 1983/84 UEFA Cup. Celtic would face Brian Clough's Nottingham Forest in the third round but lost out 2–1 on aggregate as the more experienced English side showed all their knowledge to contain a slicker, more attack-minded Celtic team. McClair played in both legs against Forest.

The following season, McClair was on target again as Celtic beat Rapid Vienna 3–0 in the now infamous Cup-Winners' Cup match. That win should have been enough for Celtic to go through but the shocking antics of the Rapid players after a missile was thrown on to the pitch, led to a play-off at Old Trafford and Celtic lost 1–0. In 1985/86, Atlético Madrid ended Celtic's interest in the Cup-Winners' Cup, while Dynamo Kiev eliminated Celtic from the 1986/87 European Cup. In total, McClair played sixteen times in Europe for Celtic and scored twice.

Yet, there was one overriding high of McClair's Celtic career that should outweigh any of the lows he suffered. The striker was one of a select band of Celtic players who, against all odds, secured one of the most dramatic title wins in the club's history. McClair will always cherish the role he played in Celtic winning the 1985/86 Scottish Premier League. Final-day title deciders are quite common in the history of Scottish football, but this one was unique. Celtic and Hearts were the two sides vying for the right to be crowned champions and the ball was in the Jambos' court. They needed just a draw against Dundee to win the title, while Celtic were hoping for a Hearts defeat plus a three-goal swing. Unbelievably, Davie Hay's side did it.

Not only did Dundee, courtesy of Albert Kidd's double, win the game 2–0, but Celtic racked up a 5–0 victory over St Mirren at Love Street to take the title on goal difference. McClair was in the thick of it. He opened the scoring with a header from Owen Archdeacon's corner and that set the tone. He was then involved in two goals for Maurice Johnston as Celtic went 3–0 ahead. Paul McStay then rammed home a stunning drive, before McClair's second put the seal on an unbelievable victory. It would however, have been worthless had Albert Kidd not scored twice to give Dundee a 2–0 win over Hearts at Dens Park. But he did and the Celtic players, including McClair, celebrated long into the night. It will always be regarded as one of the most breathtaking title wins in Celtic's history.

AND ANOTHER THING ...

His nickname 'Choccy' derives from the fact that Brian McClair's surname rhymes with the 'Chocolate Eclair' cake. He became universally known by that name, at Celtic and Manchester United, and the official Old Trafford magazine carried a popular feature called 'Choccy's Diary'.

McClair is one of a select few players who have won both the Scottish PFA Player of the Year and the Scottish Football Writers' Player of the Year awards in the same season. He managed that feat in 1986/87 after his spectacular 51-goal haul for Celtic. Other Celtic players who have been awarded both honours in the same season are Charlie Nicholas (1982/83), Paul McStay (1987/88),

Henrik Larsson (1998/99 and 2000/2001), John Hartson (2004/05) and Shunsuke Nakamura (2006/07).

During his Celtic career, McClair scored six hat-tricks for the club and all came in league games. He was top scorer for Celtic in each of his four seasons at the club and, with his best tally coming in 1986/87 when he struck forty-one times.

When he was awarded a testimonial by Manchester United in 1997, there was only one team he wanted to play against and Celtic travelled down to Old Trafford on 15 April that year for a special tribute match in his honour. United's side contained all the modern greats; Roy Keane, Eric Cantona and David Beckham among them. Keane scored for Man United, but Celtic, as they often did on these occasions, won the match 2–1, with Chris Hay scoring twice. A total of 44,000 supporters were there to honour McClair.

McClair's prolific scoring record at club level could not be replicated on the international stage. He played a total of thirty times for Scotland, but scored only twice; against Estonia in a World Cup qualifier and against the CIS (Commonwealth of Independent Russian States) at the Euro '92 tournament. That particular goal must have been something of a relief for McClair, given that it broke his Scotland duck and came almost six years after he had made his international debut. McClair, playing off the strikers, started every game at Euro '92 but never featured at a World Cup. He never made the Scotland squads for 1986 or 1990.

20

BOBBY COLLINS

117 GOALS IN 320 APPEARANCES

It's all downhill when you leave Celtic. How many times have you heard that phrase over the years? How many times has a player left Celtic and been warned that his career would only get worse from then on in? Years later, said player comes out and says he was wrong to leave Celtic and if he could turn back time he would.

Yet, there are exceptions to the rule. Henrik Larsson left Celtic after seven miraculous years and went on to win the European Cup for Barcelona and play for Manchester United. Bobby Collins, while not scaling the heights of Larsson, also showed that there can be life after Celtic by writing his name into the history books at both Everton and Leeds United. He spent ten years at Celtic and is a legend of the difficult post-war period, but Collins is fondly remembered by fans of all three clubs, most notably Leeds, where he won the Footballer of the Year award in 1965.

Collins' Celtic career was a frustrating experience for the player. The 'Wee Barra' was a wonderful talent, a gifted forward who was adored by the supporters, but the collective performance of the Celtic team in the 1950s did not lead to the honours he deserved. His overall record of 117 goals in 320 appearances shows that Collins, brave as a lion, played his own part, but only one league title, in 1954, was won by the Celtic Great.

It remains a mystery why a Celtic side containing Collins, Charlie

Tully, Bertie Peacock, Willie Fernie, Bobby Evans and Billy McPhail had such little team success, but history shows that it was one of the most disappointing eras for the club. There were a few highs in the cup competitions, not least Celtic's landmark 7–1 mauling of Rangers in the 1957 League Cup final, but Collins' record of one league title, one Scottish Cup and two League Cups still seems extremely meagre for someone of his talents.

It would also be remiss to fail to point out that Collins didn't actively seek to leave Celtic in 1958. He was a star at the club, a genuine fans' favourite who was content with life, but the Celtic board apparently needed money to finance the erection of new floodlights. Collins was sacrificed when Everton knocked on Celtic's door and dangled a cheque for £25,000. It was a huge loss for the club, but Collins enjoyed a new lease of life down south. His reputation rose despite a tough period at Goodison Park, but it was with Leeds United that Collins really made an impression on the English game. He arrived when the club was in a state of decline and helped kick-start a glorious era at Elland Road under Don Revie.

The paucity of silverware has led to a strange perception of Celtic players from the 1950s. They were a talented bunch, of that there is no doubt, yet the trophies they ought to have won simply never materialised. This should probably be a criticism levelled at the club's powerbrokers, not players. Collins should be exempt from any blame. He was an inspirational presence for Celtic during this time and would have been a major asset to any of the successful teams that followed.

FIRST GOAL

Based on the South Side of Glasgow, Pollok Juniors have always had a reputation as being one of the best clubs of their kind in

Scotland. Of the many players who represented Pollok and went on to play in the senior game, few have achieved as much as Bobby Collins. Raised in Polmadie, Collins split his football affections between Celtic, Rangers and Third Lanark. He maintains he was simply in love with football and had no real favourites in the game. He just liked watching good players.

Born on 16 February 1931, Bobby was a regular at Celtic Park, Cathkin Park and Ibrox during the early 1940s, but had also developed a talent for the game himself. Despite his diminutive frame – Bobby peaked at 5ft 4in – junior clubs started to show an interest in this tigerish young forward from Polmadie and Bobby opted for Pollok. It soon became abundantly clear that senior clubs were keeping tabs on Collins and Merseyside seemed his next destination. At seventeen, he travelled down to Liverpool to meet with Everton, who showed real interest. Collins seemed to have made his mind up that Goodison Park was his best option.

Then came a twist. Bobby suddenly had a change of heart. He wasn't sure whether Everton was the right club for him but was on the verge of taking the plunge when Jimmy McGrory made an approach and asked Collins to sign for Celtic. Everton and Celtic went to war over his signature. Two giants of the game were both determined to get their man and eventually Celtic triumphed, although Collins had to serve a six-week suspension for his role in the transfer battle. Everton officials, bitter at the public knockback, claimed: 'He's not big enough anyway.'

He eventually made his Celtic debut in a 3–2 League Cup win over Rangers on 13 August 1949. It was a huge occasion for the teenager but he was instrumental in Celtic's win, giving Rangers defender Jock 'Tiger' Shaw a torrid time. Bobby's Celtic career was off and running in the best possible fashion and his first goal arrived against Motherwell on 3 October 1949. Celtic won 2–1 at Fir Park that day and Bobby's goal would be the first of many in green and white. He made an instant impact but Celtic would end the season with nothing to show for their efforts.

100TH GOAL

Bobby Collins' Celtic career had just months remaining when he scored his 100th goal for the club. It came against St Mirren at Love Street on 8 March 1958, in a 1–1 draw and was a deserved milestone for a talented, brave and committed forward. It also sat perfectly alongside the trophies he had won for Celtic, even if his own huge personal contribution seemed out of place next to the few team medals he got his hands on.

Collins' first major honour for Celtic came in 1951 when he helped the club win the Scottish Cup. Bobby's fifteen goals made him Celtic's top league scorer that season and he also scored twice in the cup run that ended with a 1–0 win over Motherwell at Hampden. On cup final day, he played inside-right and formed a dangerous partnership with Jock Weir. Despite his early days as a wide man, Bobby would prosper as an inside-right for Celtic.

He excelled in the 1953 Coronation Cup win as Celtic beat Britain's best in some style and helped Celtic to the double in 1954, although a prolonged injury absence robbed him of a place in the cup final side against Aberdeen. 'I'd been out for ten weeks through injury, so I couldn't complain at being left out,' said Collins, who sadly never played even a minute of that triumphant cup run.

With Celtic struggling to make an impact in the league after that double-winning season, the League Cup provided some welcome solace for Collins and his teammates. He played in the 7–1 win over Rangers in 1957, just twelve months after scoring as Celtic beat Partick Thistle 3–0 in a League Cup final replay. Hampden in the Sun, then, proved to Collins' Celtic swansong.

The 100-goal milestone would come and several more goals would follow, but Collins left Celtic with plenty of spaces in his trophy cabinet. It's a shame, for he deserved to win more silverware.

LAST GOAL

It's a unique Celtic anecdote, but one that sums up the unique history of the club. In 1958, Celtic wanted to refurbish the club's home stadium. They wanted new floodlights – the biggest in the world apparently. They needed money to do all this, so a decision was made. Bobby Collins would be sold to Everton. These claims have never been fully substantiated and never probably will, but there is no doubt that Collins' departure owed much to the need for extra finance at the club. For those in charge, it seemed a good business decision. Football-wise, it was disastrous.

Collins was a bona fide superstar. His subsequent exploits with Everton and Leeds United proved this fact on a grand scale. He was one of the best players in Britain between the mid 1950s and mid 1960s. Sadly, the Celtic players and supporters were robbed of his talents for the bulk of that period. 'I had just finished a game of golf when I was told that Celtic had been looking for me and I was to phone Jimmy McGrory,' said Collins, when asked about the reasons for his Celtic departure. 'So I phoned him and he said, "Everton want to buy you, so you can go." Simple as that.'

Why would Celtic let him go? It wasn't for his football ability, so it must have been financially motivated. Collins was in his prime at that point. He had scored his 100th goal for Celtic in March 1958. Even with the summer break, he had added another seventeen to his tally by September, when he departed for Everton. In the month that preceded his exit, he scored seven times, including one against Rangers in a 2–2 league draw. His last

Celtic goal came on 10 September 1958, in a 2–0 League Cup win over Cowdenbeath, the team he trained with regularly in the early 1950s. Collins would be gone within forty-eight hours of that match.

Everton, happy to get over their bitterness from a decade previously, were thrilled to have Collins in their squad at last and he helped the Goodison Park men avoid relegation as he took to the English game like a natural. He stayed on Merseyside for close to four years, before finding a new home at Elland Road. Leeds were in dire straits at this point, but Collins became an iconic figure at Elland Road as he helped revive their fortunes. Don Revie's side were a force to be reckoned with in the 1960s and Collins led from the front, from the very start of that era. Revie called him 'the professionals' professional' and when he was voted Footballer of the Year in 1965, those Celtic directors who had allowed Collins to leave seven years earlier must have looked on sheepishly. Collins is a Celtic Great, but should have been allowed to achieve so much more.

HIGHS AND LOWS

So much has been written about Celtic's 7–1 win over Rangers in the 1957 League Cup final that you don't always know what to believe. Bobby Collins played in that match, but his contribution has since been labelled as both 'peripheral' and 'magnificent.' What's the right answer? The man himself seems happy with his display. 'I never scored in that game, although I hit the bar a couple of times and I set up a few,' said Collins. 'Remember too, I had scored in a few of the previous rounds and you have to win them before you get to the final.' He makes a good point.

That historic cup final win was the major highlight from Collins' Celtic career but he also thrived in the famous Coronation Cup victory in 1953. Held to mark the coronation of the Queen, Celtic upset the odds to reach the final at Hampden against a gifted Hibernian side. Given that the likes of Arsenal, Manchester United and Tottenham Hotspur were involved, it's safe to say the 'Battle of the Greens' from Glasgow and Edinburgh was not exactly the cup final the organisers had envisaged when the idea for the tournament was floated.

Whatever the case, Collins relished the chance to showcase his talents. His dynamite size-four boots helped him score direct from a corner in a 1–0 win over English champions Arsenal, while Manchester United were beaten 2–1. In the final against Hibs, Neilly Mochan and Jimmy Walsh were on target as Celtic, with Jock Stein in the squad, won 2–0. If the leading English clubs never knew much about Collins before that tournament, they did afterwards.

The several trophies acted as major highlights for Collins, especially the 1953/54 title, but there were real low points as well, with the 1955 Scottish Cup final replay against Clyde being the nadir. Celtic drew the original match 1–1 and Collins had played ninety minutes. Yet, when the team was named for the replay, Collins was conspicuous by his absence. No explanation was given, but it's understood that the Celtic board felt Collins had been too aggressive when charging Clyde goalkeeper Ken Hawkins, who towered above him, and decided to remove him from the team. It was hardly an inspired decision as Clyde won the replay.

'I remember meeting my dad outside Hampden, he asked me what was up and I told him I'd been dropped from the side,' recalled Collins.

He was all for going away from the game but I insisted we stay and watch it. Clyde ended up winning 1–0. I do remember that one newspaper report said that I'd played

182

very well for Celtic in the replay, even though I was sitting in the stand watching. It was nice of them all the same.

AND ANOTHER THING ...

Bobby Collins finished as Celtic's top league scorer in 1950/51 and 1951/52. In the latter season, he was an ever-present in the league for Celtic. During his Celtic career, he scored three hat-tricks, including a trio of penalties against Aberdeen in September 1953. During his Celtic career, Bobby often took the spot-kicks and, given that the power of his shot was legendary, he rarely gave goalkeepers a chance with his penalties.

His Scotland career was quite unique. He went on to make 31 appearances and score 10 goals, but there were large periods of inactivity. Collins won three caps in 1950 but then had to wait five years for his next appearance. He was then a regular in the Scotland side between 1955 and 1959, before being shunned until 1965 when he was recalled for a few games. However, Collins did score for Scotland in the 1958 World Cup against Paraguay.

He played in the senior game for twenty-four years and also played for Bury, Oldham and Shamrock Rovers in the final days of his career. Naturally, he had success and was respected at each of those clubs. When you add in his days in the junior game, Bobby played at a high level for over a quarter of a century. He moved into coaching and management circles and had spells with Huddersfield, Hull City and Barnsley. After a spell coaching in Australia, Collins returned to Leeds to become part of the youth set-up in the 1970s.

Speaking in 2003, Collins cited Henrik Larsson and Neil Lennon as the two Celtic players he admired most in the modern age. He said of Lennon: 'He works tirelessly, always passes to someone in space and gets it back again.' Collins also played for Morton in the closing years of his career and scored in his last game against Rangers at Ibrox. The Greenock side won 2–0 and Collins relished the chance to score against his old rivals.

In 1965, Bobby made an emotional return to Scotland as guest of honour at the Celtic Supporters' Association rally. He was greeted by a standing ovation from the thousands in attendance. Although he had supported Third Lanark as a boy and had attended Celtic and Rangers matches, he had developed a strong bond with the supporters, who never forgot his talents. Former teammate and Lisbon Lion, Bertie Auld, summed up the thoughts of many when he said:

Whenever Celtic supporters recall great stars from the fifties, they nominate the Wee Barra. The term 'legend' is used far too much these days, but not in the case of Bobby Collins, both as a team player and as an individual. His name is up there with the very best, and I know it's the same at both Everton and Leeds United where he was just as sensational. Bobby Collins could have graced a team in any era; he was one of British football's greatest stars.

21

JOHNNY CAMPBELL

117 GOALS IN 215 APPEARANCES

Johnny Campbell was recruited from Benburb in 1890 at the age of seventeen or eighteen; his date of birth remains a hazy detail, though given as sometime between June and December 1872. He was seen primarily as a centre forward, though it was in teaming up with Sandy McMahon on the left of the team that he, and Celtic, saw the greatest benefits.

He had two spells with Celtic. The first lasted five years before he moved south to join Aston Villa as a result of what was later described by Willie Maley as 'the stupid action of a very prominent committee man,' and there's no doubt that Celtic's loss was Villa's gain.

In his first season in England Campbell scored twenty league goals which saw him proclaimed as Europe's joint top goalscorer by the Italian sports magazine, *Guerin Sportivo*, along with Steve Bloomer of Derby County. His goals also helped Villa win the championship, finishing four points clear of Derby. And the following year he was an integral part of Villa's double-winning squad. As well as retaining the league title by a margin of eleven points from second-placed Sheffield United, Villa also won the FA Cup, beating Everton 3–2 in the final, played at Crystal Palace.

Campbell opened the scoring after eighteen minutes, and although Everton took a 2–1 lead, Villa fought back to lift the trophy. And with league results also going their way that day, it meant they were confirmed as Champions, thus being the only side ever to clinch a league and cup double on the same day.

He scored 43 goals in 53 games for Aston Villa before he was lured back to Celtic by Tom Maley, and he was delighted to return to Scotland.

Success seemed to follow Campbell throughout his career and his first season back at Celtic saw the team win the championship, with the player contributing eight league goals. And when he moved to Third Lanark in 1903, he helped them win the only league title in their history.

He played twelve times for Scotland, scoring four goals, and he captained his country on one occasion, in a 5–1 victory over Wales at Cappielow in 1902. He also twice wore the famous primrose and pink colours of Lord Rosebery, most notably in the 4–1 victory over England in April 1900. Lord Rosebery was honorary president of the SFA and the team wore his traditional racing colours in nine matches instead of the traditional blue.

FIRST GOAL

Johnny Campbell scored his first goal for Celtic in only his second competitive appearance for the club, hitting one of the team's goals in their 6–2 Scottish Cup victory away to Wishaw Thistle. It was a comfortable victory for the Celts, who took a 2–0 first-half lead in front of a crowd of around 4,000, and Campbell took just sixty seconds after the break to open his account for his new club, firing home for the first of what would prove to be 117 goals for Celtic in his two spells with the club. Campbell's debut had been in the previous round, when he played in the 3–1 replay victory over Carfin Shamrock, but he'd already pulled on the green and white stripes prior to that match.

His first run-out since joining from Benburb came against

Bolton Wanderers on 4 April 1890 during Celtic's tour of England, while he was also in the side which beat Battlefield 7–0 in the first round of the Glasgow Cup in September of that year. Willie Groves scored two of those goals, while the other five remain untraced, so it may well be that Campbell's first goal for Celtic has been forever lost in the sands of time. He would score one more goal in the team's Scottish Cup campaign that season, netting a last-minute goal in the 2–0 fifth round victory over Royal Albert at Ibrox. The SFA had ordered the match to be played on a neutral venue after the previous match had been abandoned. In the next round, played a week later, Celtic were beaten 3–0 by Dumbarton, who made it all the way to the final before losing 1–0 to Hearts.

Campbell also scored five league goals that season, including his first against Rangers in a 2–2 draw at Ibrox. The eighteen-year-old had quickly established himself as a first-team regular in the course of the 1890/91 season, when Celtic finished third in the league, but it was the arrival of Sandy McMahon in December 1890 which saw an impressive on-field partnership develop between the two men who would become Celtic's first two Century Bhoys.

100TH GOAL

The Scottish Cup would be the tournament which provided the platform for Johnny Campbell's milestone goals for Celtic. His first goal had come in that competition, and his last would as well, so it's little surprise that the goal which marked him out as a Century Bhoy also came in the world's oldest official foot-ball tournament.

Campbell netted his 100th goal for Celtic against Thornliebank on 11 January 1902 in the first round of the Scottish Cup. A crowd of just 3,000 turned up Celtic Park for the game, and they saw George Livingstone score twice before Campbell made it 3–0 from the penalty spot.

He was in his second spell at the club, having returned from Aston Villa in 1897 after two years in England, and 1901/02 saw him finish as the club's top goalscorer, albeit with a total of just twelve goals. The previous year, he and Sandy McMahon had shared that honour, with thirteen goals apiece, while the following season, which was also Campbell's last, he was once again top of the scoring charts with fifteen goals before the mantle was passed to Jimmy Quinn the following year.

Having seen off Thornliebank, Celtic made it all the way to the final for what was their fourth consecutive appearance in the showpiece occasion. Having won the trophy in 1899 and 1900, the Celts had lost out on three-in-a-row when Hearts beat them 4–3 in the 1901 final, and a year later they faced the other half of the Edinburgh divide.

The game was played at Celtic Park in front of a crowd of just over 15,000, but home advantage didn't help the Glasgow side, who went down 1–0 to Hibernian, the result denying Campbell a fourth Scottish Cup winner's medal, having also been part of the first Celtic team to win the competition back in 1892, when he scored two of the five goals against Queen's Park.

LAST GOAL

A side which could call on the collective scoring talents of Johnny Campbell, Sandy McMahon and Jimmy Quinn might have been expected to produce an abundance of goals but, in the event, only two were forthcoming in the Scottish Cup second round tie against Port Glasgow at Celtic Park on 21 February 1903.

Out of that prolific trio, only Campbell would get on the

scoresheet that day, and his goal proved to be his 117th and final goal in Celtic colours. The team won 2–0, with Thomas McDermott scoring one of only four goals he would score for Celtic in a career whose achievements never came close to matching his potential.

The victory, which came in front of just 2,000 fans, set up a quarter-final meeting with Rangers seven days later, when a somewhat bigger crowd – around 40,000 – strode into Celtic Park full of optimism, only to shuffle out despondently ninety minutes later having seen Celtic lose 3–0.

It was to be Johnny Campbell's last competitive appearance for the club, although he did play one more time, in a 2–2 draw against Dundee in the Inter City League on 2 May 1903.

Like Sandy McMahon, Campbell just missed out on wearing the green and white Hoops. He left Celtic in the middle of August to join Third Lanark, and, ironically, his first game for his new club came against the newly clothed Hoops at Celtic Park, and he helped them to a 3–1 victory in front of a crowd of 15,000, most of whom had previously stood and cheered Campbell's actions.

Indeed, it could be argued that Celtic were premature in releasing their top goalscorer, though the emergence of the two Jimmys, Quinn and McMenemy, was perhaps a natural sign that the old guard of Campbell and McMahon needed to be replaced, and they were at the heart of the club's subsequent world record of six league titles in row between 1905 and 1910.

Celtic's first season after Campbell left saw them finish third in the league, which was an improvement on the fifth place they had recorded the previous season, but the player himself had a considerably better campaign, helping his new club, Third Lanark, win the first and only league championship in their history, finishing five points clear of Celtic.

Thirds did the double on Celtic that season, winning both

league matches 3–1, though Campbell didn't find the net against his former club on either occasion. Celtic did manage to exact some revenge, however, knocking Thirds out of the Scottish Cup with a 2–1 semi-final victory, going on to beat Rangers 3–2 in the final, courtesy of a Jimmy Quinn hat-trick.

HIGHS AND LOWS

Johnny Campbell's name features in the early triumphs of Celtic Football Club and perhaps none more notably so than on 9 April 1892 when the fledgling team from the East End of Glasgow won their first major trophy, beating Queen's Park 5–1 in the Scottish Cup final.

It was a personal triumph for the striker, although the game also encapsulates one of the great strengths of Celtic at that time, with the partnership of McMahon and Campbell. Both men scored two goals that day, ensuring that the cup, which Celtic had already won in a final which was subsequently declared null and void, would have a new resting place. That would be the newly-built Celtic Park, which saw Irish politician Michael Davitt symbolically plant a sod of turf in the centre-circle of the pitch a week after the triumph.

Celtic had trailed 1–0 at half-time in the cup final, but two quick Campbell goals after the break sparked a scoring frenzy for the Celts. While McMahon would develop a taste for scoring in Scottish Cup finals, those two goals in the 1892 showpiece were the only ones Johnny Campbell would score on such an occasion, though he did win two other medals, in 1899 and 1900. Along with that treble came three league championships, again as part of the very first Celtic team to do so in 1893, a trophy they retained the following season. Campbell's last league title was in 1898.

He twice enjoyed the thrill of signing for Celtic, first in 1890 when he was still only seventeen, while he also re-signed for the club in May 1897 from Aston Villa, whom he had joined two years previously. While he would enjoy great success with the English side, winning the Double with them in 1897, his heart always remained in the East End of Glasgow. His return was hastened, in part, by the repercussions of the club's disastrous Scottish Cup exit at the hands of junior side, Arthurlie, on 9 January 1897. Celtic were obviously keen to secure his services, paying him a signing-on fee of £70, an astronomical sum of money in those days, which would be the equivalent of around £6,500 in 2010 value.

There are also some interesting footnotes to Campbell's playing career. He once scored *twelve* goals in a reserve game at Celtic Park, a feat that has never been repeated since, while he scored the very first goal at Newcastle's St James' Park, for Aston Villa, and he could also boast of being the scorer of the first ever league goal at the present Villa Park.

AND ANOTHER THING ...

The first competitive goal ever scored at the current Celtic Park came against Renton on 20 August 1892 in the opening league game of the season, courtesy of Johnny Campbell. He would score a hat-trick that day as Celtic kicked off the campaign with a 4–0 victory.

The game also saw the referee intervene with fifteen minutes remaining when Johnny Madden and a Renton player, McQuilkie, lost their tempers, the official asking both players to 'retire from the field of play.' Oh, for such genteel times again ... .

Celtic would go to win the league championship for the very first time that season, finishing a point ahead of Rangers, with

Campbell contributing 12 league goals, including one in the 3–0 victory over their rivals at Celtic Park on 29 April 1893. The Celts would narrowly miss out on a first league and cup double when they lost 2–1 to Queen's Park in the Scottish Cup final.

Campbell also found himself embroiled in legal action when he was sued successfully by a woman with whom he'd fathered a child during his time in England.

22

JOHN HARTSON

110 GOALS IN 201 APPEARANCES

Modern footballers are often accused of being out of touch with reality. The big wages, the fancy cars and the mansions ruin them, or so we are told. They can't identify with the ordinary, working-class supporter anymore. In some cases, this might be true. But don't ever level this accusation at John Hartson. You could not wish to meet a more down-to-earth, grounded, friendly individual. And he could score goals too.

Sure, big John had the money and the big house. By the time he arrived at Celtic in 2001, he was already a wealthy man. His five-year stay in Glasgow saw him earn millions of pounds more, but there was humility about him. He was a man who never forgot his roots.

That's why, when news broke that the Hoops hero was battling cancer in the summer of 2009, the entire Celtic family was hit hard. He didn't have the skill of Larsson or the genius of Moravcik, but Hartson has a special place in Celtic folklore.

He is Big Bad John; the battering ram of a centre forward who pushed defenders about and scored goals for fun. Flicks and tricks were for the more gifted players. With Hartson, you just had to get the ball into the box and wait for the fireworks.

It could all have been so different though. By now, the image of John Hartson sighted alongside Ronald De Boer at Ibrox will be etched into the minds of Rangers fans. Hartson was the one who got away, but it wasn't his fault. Wearing his official Wales polo shirt, Hartson was whisked from international duty and flown to Glasgow by David Murray for signing talks at the end of August 2000. With de Boer already signed, sealed and delivered, Hartson, then of Wimbledon, was the second part of a reported multi-million-pound double swoop by Rangers. Yet, things didn't go to plan when Rangers pulled out of the deal at the last minute, citing a failed medical. Hartson was left feeling confused and let down. He later declared it the lowest moment of his professional career.

Hartson, brought up in Swansea, started his career with Luton Town and had played for Arsenal, which made him Britain's most expensive teenager, as well as for West Ham before signing for Wimbledon in 1999 for a fee of £7.5million. By 2000, he was a man in demand but proposed transfers to Spurs, Rangers, Charlton and Coventry City all collapsed at the last minute, because of medical issues. Eventually, Gordon Strachan took a leap of faith and brought Hartson to Coventry in February 2001 and he scored enough goals to show that any perceived injury problems were not nearly as bad as had been feared. Indeed, he was playing and training constantly.

Martin O'Neill certainly had no doubts. The Celtic manager famously phoned Hartson in 2001 and told him it didn't matter if he had a hole in the heart, he was signing him. That sort of backing lifted the spirits of Hartson immeasurably and while he felt uneasy leaving Strachan behind, the striker knew straight away that he wanted to sign for Celtic.

Hartson was a revelation. Between 2001 and 2005, he won three league titles, two Scottish Cups and one League Cup, although he missed finals of both competitions. He helped Celtic to the UEFA Cup final in 2003 and was voted Player of the Year by the football writers and his fellow professionals in 2005. Under O'Neill, he teamed up with Henrik Larsson and Chris

Sutton in one of the most potent forward lines in the club's history. When O'Neill departed, Hartson played for one season under his old Coventry boss Strachan and scored twenty goals as the Hoops won the SPL and League Cup.

At the end of season 2005/06, Hartson made an emotional exit from Celtic Park to join West Brom, where he teamed up with Tony Mowbray. He had initial success at the Hawthorns but was released by West Brom in January 2008, after a short loan spell at Norwich. His last professional outing came for the Carrow Road side against Watford in November 2007. Currently waging a brave battle against cancer, John is a popular television pundit and writes a weekly newspaper column. He proved to be a fans' favourite at all eight of his professional clubs, but Celtic hold a special place in his heart. An old-school striker, they don't make them like Big Bad John anymore.

FIRST GOAL

The pressure must have been getting to John Hartson but he did his best to hide it. Upon signing for Celtic, Martin O'Neill told him that he would have to fight with Henrik Larsson and Chris Sutton for a regular place. This was no easy task. To this day, Larsson and Sutton are revered by Celtic supporters. This was the partnership that had everything; pace, power, strength, guile and personality. They struck fear into the heart of defences in Scotland and Europe and scored a combined total of sixty-six goals in their first season together. Hartson admired the duo immensely but he also wanted to play regular football. This meant making the most of every chance he got. This meant scoring goals whenever he got on the pitch. To begin with, it didn't go his way.

It may surprise some Celtic supporters to learn that Hartson failed to score in his first ten games for the club, but that's a fact.

The harder he tried, the more the goals just wouldn't come for him. Hartson, a regular scorer throughout his career, was in the midst of a personal drought. The Celtic fans backed him, but they wanted a goal from the big Welshman. They wanted to hail a new hero and see Hartson get off the mark. 20 October 2001 was the day they got their wish.

Strikers will see the irony in Hartson's hat-trick against Dundee United on the above date. Celtic battered the Tannadice side 5–1 at Celtic Park and Hartson was immense. After months of waiting for a goal, three came at once. It was a huge weight off Hartson's considerable shoulders. Taking Lubo Moravcik's pass on the edge of the box, he produced a composed finish to break his duck. 'The longer it was going on without me scoring meant that I was getting a little bit tense,' he said afterwards.

I believed I'd been playing quite well but I wasn't getting goals. As a striker that is obviously what you are judged on. It felt great to get that goal and it was brilliant to open my account with a hat-trick. It was a great ball through from Lubo and it was a real relief to see it going in.

Hartson was off and running. The two goals he added against Dundee United secured his first hat-trick as a Celtic player. He would go on to score a total of five trebles for the club. The Welsh striker finished his first season as a Celtic player with twenty-four goals and an SPL title to his name. There would be no success in the cups for Celtic, however. Hartson scored against Rangers in the Scottish Cup final but the Ibrox side edged an epic contest 3–2 at Hampden. The game marked Hartson's first goal against Rangers, but he couldn't enjoy the occasion as he sat dejected inside the national stadium at full-time.

100TH GOAL

Even now, John Hartson feels immense pride at the achievement. Larsson, Dalglish, McGrory, McClair, Nicholas, Lennox and now Hartson could be added to the list. He had just joined an elite band of players to score a century of goals for Celtic, but the big man was never going to blow his own trumpet as it sunk in that he had become the club's latest Century Bhoy. A typically opportunist goal in a 3–0 win over Falkirk took his tally to 100 and an emotional Hartson immediately spoke of his immense pride at becoming the twenty-eighth Century Bhoy in Celtic's history. 'Hitting the hundred means a lot to me – people close to me know that – and all the more so because Celtic is a club that I've got a real affection for now,' he said, immediately after the match.

Years later, Hartson talks openly about the pride he feels at hitting a ton of goals for Celtic. He was born and bred in Wales, but has a strong bond with Celtic. He knows all about the players who created history before him. James McGrory isn't just someone who is mentioned in a popular terrace chant. Hartson knows all about him. Today, when Hartson scans the list of twenty-eight players, it hits home just how big an achievement it was for him to score 100 goals in the Hoops, especially when he also thinks of the great Celtic names who didn't reach a century of goals.

'Looking back, it became a bit of an obsession for me,' he said.

Ever since I scored my first goal I wanted to hit 100 and that was always my target. I had several opportunities to leave Celtic during my time there, but I wanted to be part of the club's great tradition and history. Only twenty-eight players have scored 100 goals for Celtic. Guys like Paolo Di Canio and Pierre van Hooijdonk aren't on that list. They were fantastic players for the club and heroes for Celtic supporters, so to be in such an elite band is a fantastic honour.

Hartson wasn't finished either. After hitting the 100 mark, he scored 10 more goals that season, including the title clincher against Hearts. Just like he had done against Liverpool in 2003, he saved one of his best goals for the big occasion, slamming a swerving volley beyond Craig Gordon from twenty-five yards to seal a 1–0 win for Celtic.

Given the departure of Martin O'Neill the previous summer, it's perhaps overlooked just how good a Celtic team Gordon Strachan had in his first season in charge.

Artur Boruc was a welcome addition in goal, while Bobo Balde and Stephen McManus formed a solid partnership at the back. In midfield, captain Neil Lennon linked up effortlessly with Stilian Petrov and, in the second half of the season, Roy Keane. Shaun Maloney won the Player of the Year awards, while Shunsuke Nakamura and Aiden McGeady lit up Celtic's performances. In attack, Hartson and Maciej Zurawski scored forty goals between them as Celtic won the SPL title and League Cup. While he is best remembered for his exploits in the O'Neill era, this one season under Strachan means a lot to Hartson. He felt the pain of losing the previous SPL title on the last day more than anyone, but this made up for it.

'I scored twenty that season and it was a good season for us,' he said.

Gordon had just arrived and we had a difficult start, but the main thing was we brought the SPL trophy home after the events of the previous year. It was great for Gordon. He came in and did a wonderful job and that was a great start to his career at Celtic. My own time at Celtic was about to come to an end, but it was a great way to bow out. As a champion.

LAST GOAL

Fittingly, John Hartson's final competitive game for Celtic was marked with his final goal for the Hoops. It came at Pittodrie on 7 May 2006 and was a typically instinctive Hartson finish. Aiden McGeady's shot crashed off the bar and Hartson headed home the rebound from ten yards to give Celtic the lead in a 2–2 draw. It was Hartson's twentieth of the season and took his overall tally to 110.

Looking back, Hartson is immensely proud of that tally, especially when he points out that he missed almost an entire year of football in 2003 and 2004. But for that long hiatus, when a back problem forced him out of action for long spells, Hartson could and would have scored more than 110. Of that, there is no doubt.

'I was at Celtic for five years, but I missed the best part of a year through injury,' said Hartson.

I had back problems in 2003 and 2004 and literally missed a season of football. Basically, my record of 110 goals was achieved in four seasons and I do wonder what I would have managed to score had I stayed fit. Nevertheless, it's a record I am very proud of and I have a lot of people to thank for it. The likes of Steve Guppy, Alan Thompson, Stilian Petrov, Neil Lennon, Chris Sutton and Henrik Larsson laid on a lot of goals for me. Without that service, I would never have scored the goals I did.

Did he leave too early? Hartson isn't one for looking back and having regrets but maybe somewhere inside he wonders what would have happened had he stayed at Celtic. As it turned out, the fact Celtic couldn't guarantee regular first-team football and West Brom gave him an offer he couldn't turn down, meant Hartson was heading for England with a heavy heart.

'I left Celtic in the summer of 2006 and I had my own reasons for doing that,' he said.

I was thirty-one at the time and I'd had five great years at the club. Gordon was making changes and building a new side, so I didn't want to hang about and just be a bit-part player. I wanted to play every week and moved to West Brom. It was hard to leave Celtic after so many great times, but I have a lot of wonderful memories to look back on.

When I signed for Celtic, a lot of fans were asking why Martin was signing me. Chris and Henrik were playing so well together and the club had just won a treble, so people questioned his decision to bring me in. People were really unsure of me, so I had to win the fans over and I managed to do that. I built up a great rapport with the Celtic supporters and managed to stay in their good books by scoring goals.

HIGHS AND LOWS

Would Celtic have won the 2003 UEFA Cup had John Hartson been fit for the final? Nobody really knows, but one thing is for sure. Martin O'Neill's side would have had a better chance if the Welshman had been fit. Hartson was once quoted as saying that the searing heat of Seville would have rendered him useless. He hated playing in warm weather and the picturesque Spanish city was baking on that May evening.

We will never know what difference Hartson would have made and while his personal claim that he would have toiled in the sun is perhaps a valid one, Celtic would have been in a much stronger position had they been able to call on his talents, even as a substitute.

As it turned out, Hartson had to watch the match from the

Olympic Stadium stands. A back injury that had been plaguing him became too much as doctors ordered an operation and rest. Hartson, who scored for Arsenal in Cup-Winners' Cup campaigns, was ruled out of what should have been the biggest game of his Celtic career. He had scored vital goals against Liverpool and Celta Vigo on the road to Seville, but was wearing a suit as Celtic lost 3–2 to Jose Mourinho's side.

'I don't know if people realise this, but I missed three cup finals during my Celtic career,' he said. 'I was injured for Seville and the 2004 Scottish Cup final. I then missed the 2006 League Cup final through suspension. That was hard to take. I had to be a strong character to come back from those disappointments.'

If missing Seville was the biggest low of Hartson's Celtic career, then losing the 2004/05 SPL title on the last day of the season runs very close. Today, it still seems inconceivable that Celtic could have left Fir Park that day without any silverware. One win was all they needed to lift the SPL title for the fourth time in five years, but Scott McDonald's double gave Motherwell a 2–1 win and handed Rangers the title. With O'Neill ready to stand down as Celtic manager, it was a crushing blow for Hartson and the rest of the Hoops squad. The Scottish Cup, won courtesy of a 1–0 victory over Dundee United, softened the blow, but an era ended that day at Fir Park and Hartson felt the pain more than anyone.

Not that the lows in any way outweigh the highs of his Celtic career. His 110 goals helped Celtic to three SPL titles – two won under O'Neill and one under Strachan – while he completed a clean sweep of domestic trophies by winning both the Scottish Cup and League Cup during his time at the club. Hartson also made a habit of scoring special goals for Celtic. He loved nothing more than finding the net against Rangers and managed it a total of eight times. Given his history with the Ibrox side and that infamous medical of 2000, the Welshman took even more pleasure out of his derby goals.

Then you had the European nights. Hartson scored in the Champions League and UEFA Cup. He famously helped Celtic draw 1–1 at the Nou Camp against Barcelona when he tapped home at the back post. He was arguably offside, but Hartson didn't care. He had just scored for Celtic against Barcelona. It didn't get any better.

Or did it? Ask Hartson for the ultimate highlight of his Celtic career and the best goal he scored for the club, and the word 'Anfield' will come up in conversation. As someone who supported Liverpool as a kid, he dreamed of scoring spectacular goals at the club's legendary stadium. In those dreams, Hartson was wearing red. When he managed it for real, he was bedecked in green and white Hoops, but the elation was just as he'd imagined. His stunning, long-range goal in the 2–0 win over Liverpool in the UEFA Cup was a defining moment in his Celtic career.

'You hit one or two of them in your career,' he said.

I supported Liverpool as a kid mainly because Ian Rush was my hero and to go there, score a goal like that, such an important goal as well, was a dream come true for me. It wasn't in front of the Kop but it was in front of the Celtic fans and it was a brilliant feeling. The goal at Anfield has to be my favourite. In terms of importance, I actually felt the goal I scored in Vigo was a bigger one, but the strike at Anfield was one of my best ever and one I'll always remember.

AND ANOTHER THING ...

During his five years at Celtic, Hartson scored a total of five hat-tricks. His first came against Dundee United in October 2001 and he second came against Aberdeen in November 2002 when he scored four goals in a 7–0 rout. Hartson added trebles against Hearts, Livingston and Motherwell before leaving the club. He scored a total of eight goals against Rangers and classes his volley in a 1–0 win in season 2002/03 as his best. Taking a Chris Sutton flick in his stride, he unleashed a devastating volley past Stefan Klos from eighteen yards.

Hartson's scoring prowess wasn't limited to his days at Celtic. Throughout his career, the Welshman played for eights clubs: Luton, Arsenal, West Ham, Wimbledon, Coventry, Celtic, West Brom and Norwich. He finished with a professional career total of 205 goals. On the international scene, Hartson won 51 caps for Wales and scored 14 goals between 1997 and 2005. He is ninth on the list of all-time Wales' international scorers, with his idol Ian Rush topping the list with twenty-eight goals.

23

NEILLY MOCHAN

109 GOALS IN 268 APPEARANCES

Neilly Mochan's inclusion as one of the 28 players to have hit 100 or more goals for Celtic is undoubtedly one of the most impressive achievements of all the men who have fired their way into this exclusive band of Bhoys.

Along with John Divers and Bobby Collins, he achieved his scoring record in an era of failure for Celtic, when occasional triumphs were eclipsed by the general malaise which had settled over the club since the end of the war, the nadir of which was the near-relegation in 1948.

There were some truly gifted players at Celtic, particularly in the 1950s and into the early 1960s, names such as Charlie Tully, Bertie Peacock, Bobby Evans and Willie Fernie, but there was never any sustained success or even a resolve to build on any success that did come the team's way. The club wasn't being run properly and the manager, Jimmy McGrory, for all that the players liked and respected him particularly for his own achievements as a Celt, was not in charge of team affairs.

The chairman, Bob Kelly, ran the club and picked the team, and it often led to inexplicable line-ups and formations. Mochan had first-hand experience of this, having missed the 1955 Scottish Cup final against Clyde and subsequent replay because he'd had a fall-out with the chairman. It was no way to run a football club and Celtic suffered accordingly.

To score 109 goals in 268 appearances is an impressive achievement in any era, but to do so at a time of underachievement by the club makes it all the more laudable.

Bertie Auld, who joined the club in 1955 and became a rival to Mochan for the outside-left position, found himself working alongside a player who not only strived to improve his own game, but who was also happy to help others as well, even if he knew they were vying for his place in the team.

'He was the perfect professional for a young player to come in and learn from,' said Auld.

We had a lot of experienced players at Celtic Park at that time, and Neilly was one of them, but the most important thing was that he was always there to speak to you and give you a bit of advice.

He would always encourage you on the park. I was hitting shots as a young player, and he'd come up just right after it and say, 'listen son, that's twice you've shot and both times you've hit the near post. Looking at the angle that you're hitting it from, always hit the back post because if you don't score then at least the goalkeeper will have to save it or parry it and somebody else will get the chance to put it in.'

Neilly Mochan's Celtic connection didn't end the day he left the club as a player and signed for Dundee United. He returned to Celtic Park as a coach in February 1964 and became an integral part of the backroom team under his former teammate, Jock Stein, enjoying as much as anyone the unprecedented success which the club was now experiencing.

'Neilly was a fitness fanatic as well,' Auld said.

He was a tremendous trainer and he was a delight to work with. Every morning he was out leading everyone, even into the late 1960s. He was a tremendous example as a person and as a player.

He was also type of the character who always got the dressing room going. He was very funny. His nickname was 'Smiler', so you could picture that in a dressing room, particularly with the characters we had. He had the banter going as soon as he walked in the front door.

FIRST GOAL

Neilly Mochan began his Celtic career with a flurry of goals that saw him collect two winner's medals before he even played a game at Celtic Park.

He made his first appearance in the Hoops in the final of the 1953 Charity Cup against Queen's Park and he made an instant impact, scoring twice as Celtic won 3–1. Just a week later, on 16 May, he was in the Celtic side which beat Arsenal 1–0 and then Manchester United 2–1 in the semi-final of the Coronation Cup to help his side unexpectedly reach the final. He scored one of the goals against United but would better that in the final.

That competition, celebrating the coronation of Queen Elizabeth II, was meant to have the best teams in Scotland and England face off against each other. Celtic, who finished eighth in the league that year, were only invited because of the enormous support that their participation would guarantee.

No one expected the Hoops to reach the final, and there they faced Hibernian. It was a Battle of the Greens and one that saw Mochan hit a glorious right-foot shot into the roof of the Hibs net from thirty yards, to help secure a unique trophy triumph for Celtic. Jimmy Walsh scored Celtic's second that day near the end of the game while goalkeeper John Bonnar was outstanding for the Hoops.

Bertie Auld remembers Mochan, as a player and later as the first-team trainer during Jock Stein's reign, regaling all and sundry with elaborate descriptions of his goal every time Celtic played at the national stadium.

I heard so often about how he'd scored the winning goal in the Coronation Cup final, and any time we went to Hampden from the 1950s right up to the seventies, Neilly would talk about it, and it kept getting further and further back every time he described it.

At the finish, when we used to go out on the park to have a look at the conditions before the match, Neilly would take us over to where he'd hit his shot, and it was getting closer and closer to Johnny Bonnar's goal!

It was an impressive start for the player signed from Middlesbrough and he seemed to have a galvanising effect on the club. Celtic's immediate post-war record was dreadful, as poor as it has ever been the club's history, with their best finish in the league a lowly fifth.

Mochan's first season at Celtic Park saw them crowned champions and, just for good measure, they won the Scottish Cup as well. He can't take all the credit for that success. There were a number of talented players in the squad – as there often was at that time – along with some natural born winners such as Jock Stein, Sean Fallon and Bobby Evans, but Mochan provided pace, panache and an instinctive eye for goal that would net him twenty-five goals in that campaign.

His first competitive goal in terms of domestic competitions came at Pittodrie on 22 August 1953 in a League Cup section match. By the time he scored in the last minute, Celtic were already trailing 5–1 and on their way towards another ignominious departure from the competition before the knockout stages.

Celtic lost four of their sectional games, drawing one and winning their final match against Airdrie. They finished bottom of the section, which East Fife won, and there was nothing to suggest to the long-suffering support that this would be a momentous and triumphant season for the club. Indeed, when they lost their opening match 2–0 at Hamilton, a familiar sense of foreboding would have settled over the Hoops fans.

Celtic turned out to be worthy champions – albeit it turned out to be their only title triumph until Jock Stein's side triumphed in 1966 – and they won their last nine league fixtures, scoring thirty-two goals and conceding just four.

Mochan scored eleven of those goals, including two at Easter Road on the day the title was clinched, and while he didn't get on the scoresheet, he played his part in the 2–1 Scottish Cup final triumph over Aberdeen. Celtic finally had some trophies to display and the fans had a new goalscoring hero to acclaim.

100TH GOAL

Celtic faced St Mirren in the second round of the Scottish Cup in 1959/60 and it would take three games before the Hoops managed to progress to the next round of the competition. The first match at Love Street had finished 1–1 while the replay at Celtic Park ended 4–4 after extra-time.

Mochan had scored two goals that day, including the equaliser five minutes from time which had taken the match into extra-time, but that was just a warm-up for the third match, also played at Paradise.

Celtic won 5–2 in that game, and Neilly Mochan scored all *five* of Celtic's goals. He had put the Hoops 2–0 ahead inside the first twelve minutes, his second goal coming from the penalty spot, and he added another two before St Mirren decided to fight back. His third goal in the game was also his 100th for the club. The Paisley side reduced the deficit to two goals before Mochan scored his and Celtic's fifth of the night with nine minutes remaining.

It was an incredible individual scoring performance in a game that Fergus McCann later identified as his favourite ever Celtic game, and Mochan would go on to be the club's top goalscorer that season.

Celtic made it all the way to the final, eventually losing 4–1 in a replay to Rangers, with Mochan scoring for the Hoops.

The league campaign was another disaster, however, and the team finished eighth in the table which was topped by Hearts. The heady days of the Double which had greeted Mochan's first season at the club were now a distant memory and he now entered what would prove to be his last as a Celtic player, with little hope that better days were on the horizon.

LAST GOAL

Neilly Mochan hit the net for the final time as a Celtic player on 24 August 1960 at Rugby Park in a 2–2 draw with Kilmarnock, who had finished runners-up in the league the previous season. The goal came ten minutes from time and gave the Hoops a share of the points in a season where they would reach the dizzying heights of fourth in the table come the end of the campaign.

Mochan had played every game in the League Cup section – another failure for Celtic – but would only make one more league appearance in the Hoops, against Airdrie at Broomfield on 1 October 1960, a match that Celtic lost 2–0.

That was the infamous 'Willie Goldie' game when the team bus picked up reserve goalkeeper Willie Goldie, who was waiting at a bus stop to make his own way to the game as a supporter.

Chairman Bob Kelly was impressed by Goldie's dedication, and rewarded it by putting him into the starting XI that day for his one and only appearance for the club. Celtic lost 2–0 and it was the end of Goldie's Celtic career.

Mochan played in that game, and was probably as bemused, or annoyed as every other Celtic player, but it was an idiosyncratic way of selecting the team that was not unknown to him or his teammates.

It was also a sad way for a Celtic legend to bow out at the club, because just over a month after that farcical game at Broomfield, Mochan was off to Dundee United for the princely sum of £1,500.

He returned to Celtic Park on 10 December, lining up for his new team against the Hoops, and he helped them gain a creditable 1–1 draw, though he did not get on the scoresheet himself.

HIGHS AND LOWS

The occasional highs that came Neilly Mochan's way during his time at Celtic were spectacular ones. From scoring the winning goal in the 1953 Coronation Cup final against Hibernian, Mochan was then part of the triumphant double-winning side of the 1953/54 season.

It was an impressive achievement by a side that had been abject failures the previous season, and they only just failed to make it two-in-a-row the following year, finishing three points behind Aberdeen in second place, while the Scottish Cup was also surrendered in a replay defeat to Clyde.

Mochan's only other trophy successes came in the League Cup. Celtic won it for the first time in 1956, beating Partick Thistle 3–0 in a replay, and they would retain the trophy the following season in spectacular style.

After the 1967 European Cup triumph over Inter Milan, the 7–1 thrashing of Rangers in the 1957 League Cup final is the most famous result in Celtic's history. It remains the biggest margin of victory in a UK domestic cup final and songs were sung, and continue to be sung in memory of that day on 19 October 1957.

Neilly Mochan scored two goals that day, the first coming just before half-time to give the Hoops a 2–0 lead, and scored his second, and Celtic's fifth of the afternoon on seventy-five minutes.

It was, and still remains, a spectacular scoreline, and one which stunned Scottish football, and the players who delivered that extraordinary victory ensured their place in the Celtic history books. The team that day read: Beattie, Donnelly, Fallon, Fernie, Evans, Peacock, Tully, Collins, McPhail, Wilson, Mochan.

Sammy Wilson opened the scoring for Celtic while Willie Fernie hit number 7 from the penalty spot in the last minute, and in between Mochan grabbed his double while Billy McPhail scored a hat-trick. Oh, Hampden in the Sun ...

AND ANOTHER THING ...

Having helped Celtic secure the double in 1953/54, Neilly Mochan gained his first cap for Scotland in May 1954 in a friendly away to Norway, a match that finished 1–1. It was part of the preparations for the 1954 World Cup for which Scotland had qualified, and that would represent their first participation in the tournament, which was held in Switzerland.

Mochan was selected for the squad, and played in Scotland's two games – a 1–0 defeat to Austria followed by a 7–0 thrashing from Uruguay – with both of those teams going on to reach the semi-final of the competition.

Although most effective as an outside-left, during his time at

Celtic Mochan was also utilised as an inside-left or even a left-back, and it actually provided Celtic with some extra attacking options down that flank.

'Even when he went to left back he still looked for goals,' explained Bertie Auld. 'I know Tommy Gemmell always had a reputation for going forward and hitting them, but Neilly was like that as well.'

He remained as part of the backroom staff at Celtic Park even after Jock Stein left in 1978. He worked under Billy McNeill and Davie Hay, two men who, during their own time as players at the club, had seen the value of having someone like Mochan in the first-team set-up.

Sadly, Neilly Mochan passed away in August 1994 at the age of sixty-seven. His contribution to Celtic as a player had been impressive enough to argue, without fear of contradiction, that he was a true Celtic Great, but his devotion to the club continued many years after he hung up his boots and he always remained a favourite with supporters who saw him as one of their own.

24

FRANK McGARVEY

109 GOALS IN 245 APPEARANCES

There are very few players who can claim to have scored their first Celtic goal with their first ever touch of the ball. Barry Robson falls into that category, with the free kick he took at Pittodrie in February 2008 after coming on as a substitute and announcing his arrival at the club in spectacular style. Equally, there are not many players who can boast of scoring a goal with their last ever touch of the ball as a Celtic player, and fewer still can point to that goal being the winner in a Scottish Cup final.

Frank McGarvey can do just that, and while it is an impressive feat, growing ever more so with the passage of time, McGarvey's pride is tempered by a sense of frustration and a feeling that time was prematurely called on his Celtic career; certainly, it seems like no way to treat a Scottish Cup winner.

His diving header in the 1985 Scottish Cup final gave Celtic a 2–1 victory. It was the player's 22nd goal of that season and his 109th overall for Celtic. At the age of twenty-nine, there was nothing to suggest that his best years were behind him; they weren't, and the player himself had a strong belief in his own ability and a conviction that he could continue to make a valuable contribution to Celtic under Davie Hay.

It was money which heralded McGarvey's departure from Celtic Park. The gulf between his expectations and what the club offered could not be bridged and he moved back to St Mirren where his professional career had started some eleven years earlier.

McGarvey had already signalled his desire to play for his boyhood heroes, taking a wage cut when he joined Celtic from Liverpool in 1980. He believed, mistakenly as it turned out, that he remained a valuable member of Davie Hay's squad and that his star was on the rise after a good goalscoring return throughout the season, culminating in that winning goal at Hampden.

His career had come full circle, beginning and ending at Love Street. He was part of the youthful St Mirren side which made a powerful impression on Scottish football in the mid 1970s under the stewardship of Alex Ferguson, and he was the veteran of the St Mirren team which lifted the Scottish Cup in 1987 with a 1–0 extra-time win over Dundee United.

In between all that, he also tried his luck in England with Liverpool and found that he didn't have any. He joined a team that had won the European Cup in 1978 and 1979 and found it difficult to break into the team. At that time, players often had to endure a spell in the reserves at Anfield almost as an apprenticeship before being deemed worthy of a place in the first team. McGarvey had neither the patience nor the inclination to do so and a swift return to Scotland ensued.

He had a unique style to his play. It was languid and ungainly at times and could never be described as aesthetically pleasing, but it was effective and extremely difficult to play against. More than that, however, McGarvey had an eye for goal that was instinctive and it served him well throughout his career.

FIRST GOAL

Frank McGarvey's signing from Liverpool represented something of a transfer coup for Celtic. The club paid a then Scottish record transfer fee of £325,000 to bring the striker back to Scotland following a disappointing spell at Anfield, and twenty-four hours after joining the club, McGarvey found himself in the starting XI for the game on 12 March 1980, at home to St Mirren.

It was a fitting opposition, given that it was his former club, and it was in the black and white striped jerseys of the Paisley side that the striker had first forged a reputation in the game. One of the many impressive talents to emerge at Love Street under Alex Ferguson, McGarvey's form ensured he attracted a number of suitors and he opted for Liverpool in May 1979. Less than a year later, he was at Celtic Park.

When he joined, Celtic were eight points clear of second-placed Morton and twelve points ahead of Aberdeen, though the Pittodrie side had two games in hand. However, with two points for a win at that time, it left Billy McNeill's side looking strong favourites to retain the title they'd won the year before in Cesar's first season in charge at the club.

However, two consecutive draws, against St Mirren on McGarvey's debut and Kilmarnock, allowed Aberdeen to chip away at Celtic's lead, though the Hoops returned to winning ways with back-to-back home wins over Hibernian and Rangers, with McGarvey on the scoresheet in both matches.

His goal on sixty-three minutes in the 4–0 win over Hibs also represents his first goal in Celtic colours. It would have been a proud moment for the striker who was a self-confessed Celtic supporter, and it was part of an impressive second-half performance for the Hoops following a goalless first forty-five minutes.

If that goal, the first of 109 he would score for the club, was one for the player to savour, then his next goal was the stuff of dreams, because is there any Celtic fan in the world, and certainly any with aspirations of playing professional football, who does not dream of scoring the winning goal against Rangers?

McGarvey's dreams became a reality on the night of 2 April

1980 when he headed home the only goal of the game with just five minutes remaining. He ran to The Jungle to celebrate with his fellow fans and enjoy the acclaim which rightly came his way.

The Jungle was the heartbeat of Celtic Park in the days before the impressive and imposing all-seated arena of today was constructed, and every player wanted to perform in front of its fanatical denizens. Every player wanted to head towards the ramshackle structure after scoring a goal, never more so than in a game against Rangers, and McGarvey was no different.

'I had always thought that scoring the winner in front of the Celtic End in an Old Firm game would be amazing, and on my Old Firm debut I did it,' McGarvey recalled.

There was only a couple of minutes on the clock at 0–0 when I scored and it was one of the most incredible moments of my career. Roy Aitken crossed towards the far post and I headed it past Peter McCloy.

I couldn't believe that it had actually happened, that I had done it, and in the aftermath I think I probably broke the world record for the sixty-metre sprint. I ran from the box to the halfway line to celebrate in front of The Jungle, and it was probably the fastest I have ever moved.

Celtic, in the space of a few days, had rediscovered their winning formula and unearthed a new goalscoring hero. It makes it all the more galling, therefore, to glance at the finished table from 1979/80 and note that it was Aberdeen who ended the season as champions, one point ahead of Celtic.

100TH GOAL

Aberdeen were Celtic's main challengers for the title in the early 1980s along with Dundee United to a lesser extent. The Tannadice side had won the title in 1982/83, though it was a championship Celtic could and probably should have won.

Indeed, there remains a feeling among many of the Celtic protagonists of the time that they underachieved in terms of honours, and it could well have been five league titles in a row, rather than Dundee United and Aberdeen snatching what the Hoops players believed was rightfully theirs.

McGarvey settled quickly into life at Celtic Park, becoming the club's top goalscorer in first full season with twenty-nine goals, while he made a healthy contribution in every other season of his Celtic career.

In what would prove to be a momentous and, ultimately, bitter-sweet season for the player, he netted his 100th goal for Celtic on 8 December 1984 in a league game at Pittodrie, though it was the home side who triumphed 4–2.

Aberdeen had swept into a 3–0 lead before Celtic pulled two goals back, the second of them coming from the head of McGarvey, who bulleted home a Davie Provan cross. Any thoughts of a comeback were dispelled when the Dons restored their two-goal lead a couple of minutes later.

It was a season when the Hoops, now managed by Davie Hay, trailed Aberdeen for most of the season and finished seven points behind the defending champions in second place.

The early years of McGarvey's Celtic career had seen him fight for a place in the starting XI with George McCluskey and Charlie Nicholas. Now it was Maurice Johnston and Brian McClair who were his main challengers, though he still managed to score twenty-two goals that season, finishing just a goal behind McClair in the scoring charts.

217

It would be a season of century milestones for McGarvey. Just two weeks before he hit his 100th goal for Celtic, he also scored his 100th goal in the Premier League, becoming the first player to do so. Thirty of those goals had come for St Mirren, so it was ironic that in hitting a hat-trick against the Paisley side, he reached his impressive century.

LAST GOAL

Having managed to score 100 goals for Celtic, Frank McGarvey would only add another nine to his tally. That was not through a lack of effort on the player's part, nor was it by choice. Time was called on his Celtic career at the end of season 1984/85 and he signed off with 109 goals in 245 appearances.

His departure seemed premature at the time, and even more so now upon reflection, though it can be assumed that Davie Hay believed he already had an abundance of striking talent in McClair, Johnston and Alan McInally.

Players' careers at Celtic come and go. That is the nature, not just of the club, but of football in general, and McGarvey would have known that he wasn't going to be a Celtic player forever. He just wouldn't have expected to get dumped less than forty-eight hours after scoring the winning goal in the 1985 Scottish Cup final.

Again, the number 100 is significant, with the contest between Celtic and Dundee United also being the 100th final of the world's oldest cup competition, and it proved as dramatic as any of the previous finals.

Dundee United, still looking for their first triumph in the competition at that point – subsequently, they have won the trophy on two occasions when they beat Rangers 1–0 in 1993 and beating Ross County in 2010 – took the lead against Celtic through Stuart Beedie.

The Hoops didn't play well on the day but the collective will to win of the players, as well as the support who packed most of the sloped terraces at Hampden, ultimately proved decisive.

Davie Provan had equalised for Celtic with fourteen minutes remaining with an exquisite free kick before McGarvey supplied the winner with just six minutes of the match left. Roy Aitken, a driving force in the team that day, thundered down the right flank before delivering a cross into the box which McGarvey threw himself at, his header flashing by Hamish McAlpine in the United goal. Celtic had won the Cup again.

His reward for winning the Scottish Cup and, arguably, saving Davie Hay's job? A new contract offer that McGarvey described as 'an insult.' So after five years, he left Celtic, rejoining St Mirren where he had begun his professional career.

HIGHS AND LOWS

The biggest low of Frank McGarvey's Celtic career was undoubtedly the day he left the club. The euphoria of having scored the winning goal in a Scottish Cup final was followed swiftly by the despairing realisation that he would never again pull on the green and white Hoops.

For any Celtic player, particularly one who supported the club, it would be a sad day, and McGarvey remains convinced it was the wrong decision.

'I scored the winner in the 1985 Scottish Cup final against Dundee United with only six minutes of the game to go, and by doing so I did Davie Hay a big favour,' McGarvey said.

Davie was under a lot of pressure because of various results, and that cup final win really helped him out a lot. I wanted a four-year contract that would have kept me at Celtic Park until the end of my career but he told me he wanted rid of me. To be fair to Davie though, he wasn't a bad guy, he was just honest. He wanted to play Maurice Johnston and Brian McClair up front and that would have left me on the bench.

It was a real shock to the system because I thought that I had had a good season despite not starting a lot of games, and the news left me absolutely numb. I went from the ultimate high to the ultimate low within two days and I ended up going back to St Mirren, where I won the Scottish Cup again.

But I would never complain because I had a good career in the game won every domestic medal in the Scottish game, and that's a fantastic achievement.

In the five years leading up to that point, however, there were many highlights to savour. He scored the winner in a game against Rangers. He was part of the team which won the Scottish Cup in 1980 with a 1–0 extra-time win over Rangers, while he also gained two league championships and a League Cup winner's medal. And then, of course, there was the final honour of his Celtic career – the 1985 Scottish Cup.

He also received a standing ovation at half-time during a game at Celtic Park against St Mirren on 14 March 1981. Celtic would win that game 7–0, with McGarvey netting a hat-trick, but it was his solo goal just before half-time which had the fans rising to acclaim him.

It appeared as though he beat the entire St Mirren team – certainly he waltzed by at least half-a-dozen of them – before firing past Billy Thomson in the visitors' goal. It was a moment of sublime individual skill and the 18,100 spectators who were there savoured the moment.

He would score another hat-trick against St Mirren in November 1984 in a 7–1 victory over the Paisley side as he homed in on 100 goals for Celtic. Remarkably, the game had been tied 1–1 at half-time.

Europe proved to be a frustrating experience for Celtic and McGarvey in those years. There were some highs: knocking Ajax out of the European Cup in 1982 and beating Sporting Lisbon 5–0 at Celtic Park to overturn a 2–0 first-leg deficit, with McGarvey scoring Celtic's final goal on the night.

Unfortunately, there were also some lows. After the victory over Sporting, the Hoops were knocked out in the next round by Nottingham Forest, while the following year came the biggest European disappointment of all – Rapid Vienna.

Celtic's 3–0 home victory in the second leg appeared to have put them through to the next round of the Cup-Winners' Cup 4–3 on aggregate, but a subsequent UEFA ruling meant the game had to be replayed at a neutral venue.

The Austrians won that game at Old Trafford 1–0 and progressed all the way to the final while Celtic were left frustrated and harbouring an understandable sense of injustice. That match in Manchester was Frank McGarvey's last European appearance for the club.

AND ANOTHER THING ...

Frank McGarvey fulfilled a lifelong ambition when he signed for Celtic on 11 March 1980, becoming Scotland's most expensive player at the time. Thankfully for the club, it was his love of the green and white Hoops which saw him opt for the East End of Glasgow rather than teaming up again with his former manager, now at Pittodrie. McGarvey explained:

I signed for Celtic on the Tuesday and then played against St Mirren on the Wednesday night. But on the Monday before I went up to Glasgow, Alex Ferguson tried to get me to sign for Aberdeen.

They offered me more money than Celtic, and I was already taking a £175 per week pay-cut by leaving Liverpool, but it wasn't a difficult decision for me to make at the time.

I had been a Celtic supporter all my life and jumped at the chance to play for the club. Ferguson told me that if I went to Pittodrie and Aberdeen hadn't won anything within two years then he would let me go on a free transfer. That's how confident he was in his ability to turn them into a successful team.

Ferguson was a great manager, and I had played under him at St Mirren, but there was just no way I could let a move to Celtic pass me by, and even now I have absolutely no regrets about my decision to go there because I had a brilliant time there and I can't complain.

If I was faced with the same decision today I would do it again. Although, from a purely professional point of view I would probably say that I should never have left Liverpool.

Although I was in the second team and desperate to be playing first-team football, most of the players then had all spent at least a season or two in the reserves waiting their chance. But like any young boy I was eager to make my mark, and when Celtic offered me the chance I had to go. If I hadn't I would always have been wondering 'what if.'

25

JOE CASSIDY

104 GOALS IN 204 GAMES

Joe Cassidy lived a life less ordinary. His Celtic story is a compelling one that sums up the life and times of a great. He may not be held in the esteem of Henrik Larsson and James McGrory, but those who know their history will understand his impact at the club. Not that Cassidy's Celtic career was straightforward. In fact, it was quite the opposite.

Cassidy originally signed for Celtic in 1912 but football was put on the backburner while he fought in the First World War, for which he was awarded the Military Medal. It wasn't until 1919 that Cassidy's Celtic career really took off. Prior to that, the diminutive striker had only made fleeting appearances for Celtic but he returned from his time in the forces and became one of the most prolific strikers in the club's early history.

Cassidy's first goals came for Celtic in season 1918/19, but it wasn't until the 1920/21 campaign that he really demonstrated his scoring prowess, with 21 goals in the league and Scottish Cup. Cassidy's stock was rising at this point and he bettered that hugely impressive tally by grabbing 33 goals in 1922/23. In the following campaign, he hit 25. Cassidy had made his mark at the club in some style.

There were honours to go with Cassidy's goals as well. He played his part in two league titles – 1918/19 and 1921/22 – and was the inspiration as Celtic lifted the Scottish Cup in 1923. He scored eleven goals in the tournament that season, including the winner against Hibernian in the final. It remains a club record to this day. No other player has scored more Scottish Cup goals in one season for the club.

What kind of player was Cassidy? He stood at only 5ft 7in but was a better header of the ball than many men who stood over 6ft. The great McGrory was famed for his heading ability, but someone must have given him good lessons in that particular skill. Someone did; his name was Joe Cassidy. McGrory later named his inspiration in his all-time Celtic XI, which shows the regard in which Cassidy was held.

Cassidy died at the age of just fifty-two but had made an impression wherever he travelled in life. Few Celtic players, if any, experienced the kind of existence Joe did, but he was never short of a story to tell. Celtic fans of that generation always viewed him as an intelligent attacking player but that only tells half the story. Cassidy was a unique human being and deserves a prominent position in Celtic's history.

FIRST GOAL

Joe Cassidy's timing was impeccable. It was December 1918, Celtic were in the middle of a championship challenge and were looking for reinforcements. Cassidy provided that when he strolled back into Scotland unexpectedly just as 1919 was about to dawn and declared himself ready and able to play again for Celtic. He wouldn't have to wait long for his second 'debut', which came on New Year's Day, 1919, in a 1–1 draw with Rangers. Jimmy McMenemy was the man on target for Celtic.

With the Scottish Cup suspended, the league was Celtic's main focus. They had been dominant in Scottish football again, winning four consecutive titles between 1914 and 1917, but had come up short in 1918, losing out to Rangers by a solitary point. This meant that the next title was even more crucial and Celtic won by the finest of margins. Again, just a point separated Celtic and Rangers at the top of the table.

Cassidy flitted in and out of the Celtic side upon his return. Understandably, those players who had brought so much success to Celtic during the war years were ahead of him in the pecking order, but he still made a contribution. Cassidy's first goal came against Clydebank in a 3–1 home win on 11 January. Later that season, he would also scored a crucial double against Queen's Park to give Celtic a 2–0 win and kick-start a six-game winning streak that eventually gave them the upper hand over Rangers in an engrossing title race.

100TH GOAL

Joe Cassidy scored eight hat-tricks for Celtic. Two of those trebles came in the Scottish Cup and six came in the league, one of which also marked the occasion of his 100th goal for the club. It speaks volumes for the consistency of Cassidy's striking that he managed to hit the century in the space of five years. For three consecutive seasons, between 1921/22 and 1923/24, he finished as Celtic's top scorer.

His final overall tally of 104 would suggest that his final season brought the milestone and that guess is correct. Hearts were the opponents on 26 February 1924, and Cassidy would go on to score a hat-trick in a 4–1 win at Celtic Park. His second goal that day was his 100th for Celtic. Number 101 would follow soon after.

Celtic never won any silverware that season, so Cassidy had to make do with this personal achievement. He would have been thrilled to add a team trophy to that historic season, but Cassidy had to be content with the achievements of previous years. He finished his Celtic career as the proud owner of two league championship medals, 1918/19 and 1921/22, and one Scottish Cup medal from 1923.

LAST GOAL

Joe Cassidy left Celtic to sign for Bolton Wanderers on 9 August 1924. It was one week before the start of season 1924/25 but Cassidy had played his last game for Celtic. His final competitive outing for the club came against Hibernian in a 1–1 draw on the last day of the previous season. His final goal arrived on 5 April 1924, when Celtic beat Ayr United 3–0 at Celtic Park. It was quite a low-key way for a great striker to finish off his Celtic career.

Understandably, given his intelligence and knack for scoring important goals, there were no shortage of suitors for Cassidy and he made the short trip south to join Bolton for a fee of £4,500. Just over a year later, he was off to Wales for a stint at Cardiff City. By the summer of 1926, he was back in Scotland with Dundee.

Two years later, he signed for Clyde and then moved on to the Irish League with Ballymena in 1929. There, he won the Irish Cup with a 2–1 win over Belfast Celtic. Joe also had spells with Dundalk and Morton before calling time on his professional career some twenty years after it had started. He loved life on the road, as we can see by his many moves post-Celtic. Yet, Celtic Park was always the place he called home. Joe Cassidy died on 23 July 1949.

HIGHS AND LOWS

The 1923 Scottish Cup belonged to Celtic. More specifically, the 1923 Scottish Cup belonged to Joe Cassidy. If ever a man won a tournament on his own, this was it. In total, Celtic scored thirteen goals then won the trophy. Adam McLean and Andy McAtee grabbed one apiece, while Cassidy scored eleven of them. He was in his prime as a striker.

His *annus mirabilis* in the Scottish Cup began with a hat-trick against Lochgelly United in the first round 3–2 win on 13 January 1923. Hurlford were up next, later in the same month, and again Cassidy grabbed all of Celtic's goals in a 4–0 rout. East Fife visited Celtic Park in the third round and Cassidy was again on the mark, this time with a double in the 2–1 win. Yet, when Raith Rovers travelled through to Glasgow on 24 February, Cassidy decided to give opposition defences a break. McLean was Celtic's scorer in a 1–0 win. Motherwell were drawn against Celtic in the semi-final and Cassidy and McAtee were on target in a 2–0 win. Joe's goal came within the first minute.

Then came Hibs, who had cruised into the final with barely a problem. The Edinburgh side had yet to concede a goal in that season's tournament, but they had also yet to face a striker of Cassidy's stature. It was a tight game, but Cassidy, like he had so often that season, proved to be the difference. His goal came in the sixty-fourth minute, when he planted a header beyond the reach of Hibernian goalkeeper Bill Harper. Celtic were in dreamland and Cassidy had been the inspiration for the club's first Scottish Cup triumph since 1914.

That was undoubtedly his greatest spell in a Celtic strip. Yet, it was his only Scottish Cup triumph as a Celtic player and that would have rankled with him. Indeed, his tally of three major honours from his 200-plus appearances ought to be more. His talents deserved greater success. Other highlights include a double in a 2–0 New Year's Day win over Rangers in 1921. However, he didn't always have the best of fortunes against the Ibrox side. The following season, he was one the losing side in a 3–1 defeat at Ibrox and went home with a broken jaw for his troubles.

AND ANOTHER THING ...

Joe Cassidy's nomadic existence in his final days as a professional can be summed up with the fact that his first four children were born in Scotland, England, Wales and Ireland. In keeping with this cross-border theme, it should be noted that Joe represented both the Scottish and Irish Leagues in competition. Cassidy also represented the Scotland national side on four occasions between 1921 and 1924. He scored once – against Northern Ireland at Windsor Park in a 2–0 win on 26 February 1921 – and made his final Scotland appearance against Wales in February 1924.

There are, in actual fact, two men by the name of Joe Cassidy who have represented Celtic. Cassidy the Century Bhoy followed in the footsteps of his namesake, who had played for Celtic between 1893 and 1895. The two men both filled the inside-left position for Celtic on many occasions and Cassidy the first also had a hugely impressive scoring rate. He hit 17 goals in 36 games before leaving for Newton Heath.

26

BOBBY MURDOCH

102 GOALS IN 484 APPEARANCES

'Jinky was the best entertainer,' said Bertie Auld, who partnered Bobby Murdoch in the heart of the Celtic midfield during the glory days of Jock Stein's reign, 'but as far as I'm concerned, Bobby Murdoch was the best player.'

Murdoch had joined Celtic in 1959, and would have made his first contact with a man who would play such a pivotal role in his later footballing career. Jock Stein was in charge of Celtic's reserves at that time, and his coaching and training methods, revolutionary as they were in those days, proved an instant hit with his young charges.

That those 'revolutionary' methods involved using a football throughout a training session as opposed to just getting the players to run about for a couple of hours shows the archaic attitude prevalent in the game at that time. Stein was a man of vision, a coach well ahead of his time and he would go on to prove that at Celtic in the 1960s and 1970s.

In 1959, however, the very fact that he dispelled the notion that a football was only to be seen at a match on a Saturday, instantly identified him to be so.

Sadly for Murdoch and for Celtic, Stein left in 1960 to take up the manager's job at Dunfermline Athletic, escaping the malaise which seemed to loiter permanently at Celtic Park.

Goalscoring legend Jimmy McGrory was the manager, but

chairman Bob Kelly picked the team, and that dynamic at the club proved disastrous.

Celtic were still continuing to identify and bring through exceptional players. Murdoch was one as were John Clark, Billy McNeill, Jimmy Johnstone and Bobby Lennox to name but a few, but there was no sense of direction in the team or at the club, and had it not been for Stein's return in 1965, most, if not all of those players, along with a whole host of others, would have left to fulfil their promise elsewhere, leaving Celtic in the doldrums where they had been more or less consistently since the end of the Second World War.

By 1965, Bobby Murdoch was a first-team regular, having first broken into the team three years previously, but it was Stein who made him a world-class player. Whether it had been something the manager had identified when he'd first watched the teenage player back in 1959, or whether it was something he'd noticed as Murdoch performed in the Celtic first team, the decision to move the player into a more withdrawn midfield role proved an inspirational one.

Murdoch was not a holding midfielder in the modern sense of the word – he scored 102 goals, after all – but Stein realised that he could utilise his talents by allowing him to see the play in front of him, rather than having him in a more forward role.

Putting the combative, skilful and experienced Bertie Auld in alongside Murdoch proved another masterstroke and, together, they became the fulcrum of Celtic's play, with devastating effect.

'Jock decided that Bobby was better looking onto the play rather than being beyond the play,' Auld explained.

We had a great understanding in midfield and it didn't matter where he was playing or who he was up against, he had a telling part in the game.

He scored so many magnificent goals at crucial times

from outside the box with either foot. People think he was right-sided but he scored goals with his left peg as well.

When Bobby Murdoch played, Celtic played. That is surely a fitting epitaph for one of the greatest players ever to have worn the famous green and white Hoops. Sadly, it is an epitaph because Murdoch died on 15 May 2001 at the age of just fifty-six. He was the first of the Lisbon Lions to pass away and his death, mourned by the entire Celtic family, was felt most acutely by the men he had played alongside and who had become a band of brothers in the intervening years.

'He was a beautiful guy and he never ever changed,' said Bertie Auld. 'And I don't think I ever heard him say anything about himself.'

FIRST GOAL

Just six days short of his eighteenth birthday, Bobby Murdoch made his debut for Celtic on 11 August 1962 in a League Cup sectional match against Hearts. He announced his arrival with a goal after just seven minutes and it put the Hoops on the road to a 3–1 victory. He would also score when the teams met again at Tynecastle two weeks later, though this time Celtic went down 3–2, with a future teammate of Murdoch's, Willie Wallace, getting two of Hearts' goals.

Murdoch's chance in the first team was inevitable and manager Jimmy McGrory would have been keen to utilise the strength and power of a young man who began his career as an out-and-out forward.

Whether that chance would have come against Hearts had John Divers not forgotten his boots and been dropped for the game remains open to speculation, but Murdoch certainly grabbed the opportunity and kept his place for the remainder of the League Cup games, though Celtic failed to qualify from the section.

That first season, Murdoch made a total of 31 appearances for the club, including 19 in a league campaign that saw Celtic finish fourth in the table, and the teenager hit 11 goals, including his first hat-trick for the club in the 6–0 Scottish Cup win over Gala Fairydean, and his first goal against Rangers, equalising for Celtic in the Scottish Cup final.

Unfortunately, after that 1–1 draw, it was Rangers who lifted the trophy with a 3–0 victory in the replay.

It wasn't a great period for Celtic, with the club carrying on in the early 1960s where they'd left off the previous decade, with a lot of talented players but a lack of cohesion and organisation, and manager Jimmy McGrory, while respected by all the players, unable to assert his control over team matters in the face of boardroom interference. That would only change with the arrival of Jock Stein in 1965, and it was to the benefit of the club that it did.

It was also Stein who fully appreciated the talents of Bobby Murdoch, but in a midfield role and, in playing him alongside Bertie Auld, created one of the strongest and most dominant central midfield pairings in European football at that time.

100TH GOAL

Just over ten years after he'd struck his first goal for Celtic, Bobby Murdoch scored his 100th. It came at Cappielow on 9 September 1972 in a 2–0 league win over Morton and it was a penalty.

Murdoch had scored from the spot in the opening game of the season when Celtic beat Kilmarnock 6–2, and he was on target again after the Hoops won a twenty-first minute penalty against Morton. By then they were already 1–0 up, Murdoch having given them the lead on thirteen minutes.

It was to be the player's last full season at the club, but one in which he played forty games as Celtic clinched their eighth league title in a row, and while he only scored seven goals, his contribution to the club's success was a vital one.

The signing of Stevie Murray from Aberdeen, a box-to-box midfielder, at the end of the season served as a possible indication as to the type of player Stein was looking for in the centre of the park, but Murdoch remained peerless in being able to dictate a game and pick out a pass, and there's no doubt he could have continued to do a job for Celtic.

Stein's side had secured league title Number 8 with an impressive burst of form in the final seven matches of the season, scoring twenty-three goals and conceding just one as they finished a point ahead of Rangers.

The cup competitions provided the chance of a domestic treble, but Hibernian beat them 2–1 in the final of the League Cup while Rangers won the Scottish Cup with a 3–2 victory over the Hoops

To have reached 100 goals was an impressive personal achievement for Bobby Murdoch, given that he spent the majority of his Celtic career as a midfielder, though even if he was aware of it at the time, his innate modesty would probably have muted any celebrations.

LAST GOAL

That same 1972/73 season also saw Bobby Murdoch score his last ever goal for his beloved Hoops in a 1–1 home draw against Partick Thistle on 10 February. It came twenty minutes from the end of the game and cancelled out Thistle's first-half opener.

Murdoch was one of four Lisbon Lions who played in the team that day, along with Billy McNeill, Jimmy Johnstone and Bobby Lennox, while in the Thistle team was Stevie Chalmers, the man who'd scored the winning goal in Lisbon back in May 1967.

Bobby Murdoch had started life as a centre forward and it was in this position that he first pushed his way into the Celtic first team, but it was in a more reserved role that he really showed his class. It served Celtic well over a number of years, though whether he would have remained at the club if Stein hadn't returned as manager is doubtful.

Certainly at that time, other players such as Billy McNeill were contemplating their futures with a club that was seemingly content to drift along in relative mediocrity, and it's hard to imagine that there would not have been a steady stream of top English clubs knocking at the doors of Celtic Park if there had been the slightest hint Bobby Murdoch was for sale.

In Murdoch's first season, the club lost a top-class midfielder in Pat Crerand when then Celtic chairman, Bob Kelly, sold him to Manchester United. He would have proved to be a perfect foil for the younger man in midfield, and Stein, recognising the need for steel as well as sublime skill, brought Bertie Auld back to the club in 1965. Crerand, meanwhile, proved his quality as he helped Manchester United win the European Cup a year after Celtic had lifted the trophy.

Auld left Celtic in 1971 and his midfield partner followed him out the door two years later, heading south, where Auld had gone east to join Hibernian. For the older of the two men, Murdoch's exit from Celtic Park came as a complete surprise to him.

'I couldn't see them letting him go to Middlesbrough because he was still a young man and a magnificent player,' said Auld.

And it was there for him because John Clark had started to get one or two knocks, and problems with his cartilage.

Bobby would have been the ideal player to play at the back because he read the game so well. He didn't give the ball away easily and he was a force to be reckoned with. I honestly believed he would have become Scotland's Beckenbauer.

However, it seemed as though Scottish football held no more challenges for Murdoch, something both player and manager acknowledged at the time and it was a reluctant parting of the ways. His poignant comments years later on the European triumph hint at the truth of that.

Murdoch said: 'When we gathered for the first meeting the next season, Jock said, "For some of you football will never be the same again." He wanted to provoke us into proving him wrong, but it turned out to be right.'

HIGHS AND LOWS

There are so many highlights of Bobby Murdoch's Celtic career that it's difficult to focus on any in particular, though the obvious one is the 1967 European Cup triumph over Inter Milan.

Here was a player who also won 8 League Championships, 5 Scottish Cups and 6 League Cups, and who scored 102 goals in 484 appearances for his team.

That, perhaps, would always have been the highlight for the player himself; that he was Bobby Murdoch of Celtic Football Club and had managed to pull on the green and white Hoops so many times.

He always remained, first and foremost, a supporter, and the fans retained a special affection for a man they recognised as one of their own. His untimely passing, in 2001, was mourned by his family, friends and by the fans who had watched him over many years.

There were disappointments in the course of the fourteen years he spent at the club, though in listing his impressive roll of honours, the first thing to note is that he just missed out on the nine-in-a-row. He had been there before Jock Stein's arrival but became a pivotal figure in Celtic's subsequent success under the manager, and it would have been fitting if he'd stayed another season at the club and got the full set of league winner's medals, because if any player deserved it, then it was Bobby Murdoch.

Jimmy McGrory had likened him to another Celtic Century Bhoy, Alec Thomson, for his intelligence on the park. Jock Stein always acknowledged the importance of Murdoch's talent to his team's success, while Jack Charlton admitted it was his best ever signing when he took the player to Middlesbrough in 1973.

It can sometimes be difficult to imagine how one man in a field of twenty-two can be so influential, but those who played alongside Bobby Murdoch, and those who were lucky enough to watch him from the terraces in his prime, know what that means.

He could control a game with his passing, dictating the tempo of the game as well as where the action would be, and players such as Bobby Lennox, Stevie Chalmers, Willie Wallace, John Hughes, Joe McBride and Jimmy Johnstone, among others, thrived on the service he provided.

He was voted Scottish Player of the Year in 1969 but would only gain twelve caps for his country. Scotland's shame? It was certainly a mystery.

He was a goal-maker as well as a goal-taker, and some forty years on, Celtic fans of a certain vintage still wait to see a midfield partnership which can rival that of Murdoch and Auld.

It was his shot which was steered into the Inter Milan net by

Stevie Chalmers that sunny day in May 1967, and he was happy to let his teammate take all the credit.

'People told me, "It was going in anyway," but it had more chance of going for a throw-in,' Murdoch once said with characteristic modesty of the goal. 'Steve got a great touch to turn it in.'

AND ANOTHER THING ...

'Bobby Murdoch was the player that everybody – opposition as well as the squad of players we had – respected,' said Bertie Auld. 'We were all respected for our individual ability but Bobby stamped his authority on so many games.'

So speaks a teammate and a friend, but Bertie Auld also speaks with the wisdom of a man who knows the game inside out, and who played alongside or against some of the best players ever to grace a football field. He was no bad player himself and had a ringside seat to appreciate the God-given talents of Bobby Murdoch.

But Auld and his Celtic teammates, were not alone in appreciating what the quiet, unassuming Rutherglen boy brought to the game.

After Celtic's 1967 European Cup triumph in Lisbon, Inter Milan manager Helenio Herrera declared that, 'Bobby Murdoch is my complete footballer.'

It was Jack Charlton who signed Murdoch for Middlesbrough – his first signing for the club – and it was one he never regretted making.

'I'd played against him for Leeds when he scored at Hampden to send us out of the European Cup... but I forgave him for that!' said Charlton.

Bobby was an amazing passer of a ball who could drop a ball on a sixpence from any distance and, although I've had players who covered more ground, I never worked with anyone who could strike the ball as well as he could. His delivery into the box was always perfection but then again he was a 100% footballer … so full of class.

But even though he was magnificent for us, I knew he could be even better. Secretly, I always used to hope that someone would kick him early in the match because, when that happened, he always stepped up a gear. He was a great, great player and real favourite with the fans at Ayresome Park.

And a young player taking his first steps in the game at that time, Graeme Souness, was also in awe of a truly great player. Souness said:

We all learned something from him. He was very much the guv'nor. Bobby had a European Cup medal with Celtic as well as winning everything that could have been won in Scotland.

Everyone looked up to him, not just all the Middlesbrough players but all the lads who played against him down there. He still passed the ball better than anyone and he could look after himself on the pitch, too. Bobby wasn't someone who pulled you aside and said: 'You should be doing this' or 'You should be doing that'. Instead, he did it all by example.

Jock Stein once said of Bobby Murdoch: 'As far as I am concerned he was just about the best player I had as manager.' And having managed some great players, that is as fine a tribute to Bobby Murdoch's talents as it's possible to pay.

27

ALEC THOMSON

101 GOALS IN 451 APPEARANCES

In the list of twenty-eight players who scored 100 or more goals for Celtic, Alex Thomson is probably one of the least known. He played for Celtic between 1922 and 1934, making an impressive 451 appearances for the club, but he played in an era that wasn't the most successful.

His contribution, while more than impressive when you consider the fact he also scored 101 goals in those 451 appearances, was eclipsed by more famous teammates, most notably Patsy Gallacher and then Jimmy McGrory, both of whom also hit over 100 goals for Celtic.

And in that period, there is really only one Thomson that fans remember and talk about, though it is as much because of the tragedy of his short life as it is because of his undoubted talent on the football field.

Alec Thomson was one of three players of that surname who plied their trade for Celtic in the 1920s and early 1930s, and he was certainly the most fortunate of the three.

While he lived until the age of seventy-four, the other two men were not so fortunate. Goalkeeper John Thomson joined Celtic four years after Alec and made his debut in February 1927 against Dundee. He was brave and fearless, while also being graceful and agile, and he was already Celtic's first-choice keeper – and Scotland's – by the time of his death in 1931.

The third of the Thomson's was Bertie, an outside-right who played for the club between 1929 and 1933. He made his debut against Cowdenbeath in November 1929 and went on to make 131 appearances for the club, scoring 30 goals. His finest moment came in the replay of the 1931 Scottish Cup final against Motherwell, when he scored two goals in the 4–2 victory.

He had skill in abundance, but apparently disdained training, which provoked the ire of manager Willie Maley. After he refused to do extra training because of his 'unsatisfactory play and physical condition,' Bertie Thomson was suspended *sine die*, eventually leaving for Blackpool in August 1933. He died in September 1937 of heart trouble at the age of just thirty.

Celtic, at that time, had more than their fair share of tragedy to contend with, and as well as the untimely deaths of the two Thomsons, John and Bertie, the club also lost Peter Scarff, who passed away in 1933 at the age of twenty-five from tuberculosis.

While playing for Fife side, Wellesley Juniors, Alec Thomson was actually invited for a trial with East Fife, but they decided they didn't need him – he ended up being called into action as a linesman for the trial game – but East Fife's loss was most certainly Celtic's gain.

The fact that he played so many times for Celtic indicates that he was a model of consistency for Willie Maley's side, and the manager was always happy to have him in his team.

He may not be a name familiar to many Celtic supporters, but the history books record his achievements and contribution to the cause, and it remains a formidable one.

FIRST GOAL

Alec Thomson made his debut for Celtic a month after signing for the club, playing in the 1–0 victory over Clyde at Shawfield on 11 November 1922. He joined a team which had won the league championship the previous season, but it was to be a disappointing campaign, in which Thomson played nine times as Celtic finished third in the table.

There was the consolation of a 1–0 Scottish Cup final victory over Hibernian, although Thomson didn't play in that game. The goal that day was scored by Joe Cassidy and he would also be on target when Thomson got his Celtic goals tally up and running on 7 April, 1923.

It was the new Bhoy who opened the scoring against Hearts after just ten minutes, and Cassidy made it 2–0 for Celtic fifteen minutes later. Hearts reduced the deficit in the second-half but Celtic held on to win the match.

As the 1920s beckoned, it looked like Celtic and Rangers were taking it in turns to win the league, though as the decade progressed, it was the Ibrox side who began to assert their dominance, much to the dismay of a Celtic support who had enjoyed an abundance of success in the first twenty years of the twentieth century, with eleven league titles and seven Scottish Cups to celebrate.

Thomson arrived in 1922, blessed with superb control and passing ability that Willie Maley saw as ideal to augment the peerless talents of Patsy Gallacher. A year later, Jimmy McGrory arrived to provide the goals, which he did in abundance, so there were ingredients there for a successful side.

What Maley hadn't found was an impregnable defence which had been the bedrock of his previous great Celtic teams. Where Young, Loney and Hay provided a barrier at the back during the six-in-a-row era, the Celtic team of the 1920s could not call upon a similar backline.

So while there were still triumphs, they were not achieved consistently and Celtic would only win two league titles in the 1920s, a poor return for a club so used to success, while the

Scottish Cup was won on three occasions during that same period.

Thomson's first goal for Celtic was also his only goal for season 1922/23, while the following year he netted three, but it was his longevity at Celtic Park – he was there for twelve years – that saw him slowly but surely rack up the goals that would see him eventually pass the 100-mark, though in no season did he finish as Celtic's top scorer.

That was hardly surprising, however, given that a certain James Edward McGrory was in the team at the same time.

100TH GOAL

It took Alec Thomson until his last season at Celtic before he finally scored his 100th goal for the club. It came against Queen's Park on 30 September 1933 and helped Celtic to a 3–1 win over the Hampden side.

It came in the sixty-ninth minute of the match and was the final match of the afternoon in front of a crowd of just 5,000 at Celtic Park.

The 1930s would prove to be as difficult for the club as the previous decade had been, with only two league titles and three Scottish Cups to show for their efforts, and Alec Thomson bowed out at the end of 1933/34 without any last winner's medals to show for his efforts, Celtic finishing third in the league and being knocked out of the Scottish Cup by St Mirren.

The season was probably most remarkable for the fact that it was the only season in twelve, stretching from 1925 through to 1937, when Jimmy McGrory wasn't the club's top goalscorer. He netted 18 that season compared to Frank O'Donnell's 27, while Thomson scored just two goals, including that 100th one against Queen's Park. His other goal would also prove to be his last for the club.

The most goals Alec Thomson ever scored for Celtic in one season was nineteen in season 1925/26, when he helped Celtic win the title as they finished eight points clear of second-placed Airdrie.

Yet the goals continued to add up, though it would be interesting to discover how many goals he created during the time he was at the club. Unfortunately, there are no statistics for assists in that period, but it's likely that his assists would outweigh his goals.

Certainly, he was a tireless presence in the Celtic side, and could conjure up mazy runs in the great tradition of Patsy Gallacher, while he had an ability to see a pass that would later be replicated and emulated by Bobby Murdoch in the 1960s.

Thomson also had the perfect outlet for his crosses in the powerful and fearless Jimmy McGrory and the winger, in providing so many goalscoring opportunities for his colleague, was also, without realising it, helping to create Celtic history at the time.

LAST GOAL

Having reached a century of goals, Alec Thomson would only score one more goal for Celtic and it came on 2 December 1933 in a home league match against Airdrie. Thomson opened the scoring that day, netting after just seventeen minutes, and while only 5,000 supporters had witnessed his 100th goal for the club, there were even fewer to see goal No.101 and his final one in the green and white Hoops.

A crowd of just 3,000 gathered at Celtic Park for the match, a sign of Celtic's form at the time, as well as an indication of the harsh economic conditions in Glasgow then.

Alec Thomson would play a further thirteen games for Celtic

before his final appearance in the second-last league game of the season against Hamilton Accies at Celtic Park.

The Hoops won that game 5–1, though the fact they were a massive 19 points behind league leaders Rangers meant that a crowd of just 2,000 trundled through the turnstiles that day.

Thomson had been a faithful servant of the club for twelve years and had been a consistent performer throughout that time. He made a total of 451 appearances for the club, which puts him in the top twenty all-time list for the club – he is Number 16 –, while he managed to get over the 100-goal mark – just – before he left for Dunfermline in June 1934. He played several times against Celtic but he didn't manage to score against his former club.

HIGHS AND LOWS

The 1925 Scottish Cup final between Celtic and Dundee will be forever remembered as the 'Patsy Gallacher Final' for the extraordinary goal the Irishman conjured up to help bring the cup back to Paradise.

In *The Story of the Celtic*, Willie Maley stated:

> For twenty minutes they [Dundee] held out, and when they were at last beaten it was by an effort which will never be forgotten by those who were privileged to be present.
>
> Patsy Gallacher was the hero of the incident. He obtained possession of the ball and beat man after man by a twisting and turning movement which took him right in on goal, and he finished it by literally carrying the ball into the net.

Gallacher apparently somersaulted over the Dundee defenders with the ball between his feet and into the back of the net.

Maley continued:

Friend and foe cheered alike. It was one of these efforts which have to be seen to be appreciated, and it was with difficulty, so I was told after the game, that the Dundee players refrained from joining in the tribute to that wonderful little player.

Alec Thomson would not have refrained from congratulating his teammate, nor Jimmy McGrory who provided the winning goal with three minutes of the match remaining. It represented Thomson's first winner's medal as a Celtic player, and he would add further Scottish Cup medals in 1927 and 1931, and also won a league title in 1926.

If those were occasional high points, then the low point of Alec Thomson's time at Celtic, and one of the lowest moments in the history of the club, came on 5 September 1931 when Celtic faced Rangers in a league game at Ibrox.

Thomson was in the team that day when his teammate, fellow Fifer and namesake, John Thomson, suffered fatal head injuries while diving at the feet of Rangers forward Sam English.

The young Celtic goalkeeper, just twenty-two years old, died later that same day in the Victoria Infirmary, Glasgow, and the Celtic players, management and supporters were left devastated.

'His merit as a goalkeeper shone superbly in his play,' wrote Willie Maley.

Never was there a keeper who caught and held the fastest shots with such grace and ease. In all he did there was balance and beauty of movement wonderful to watch. Among the great Celts who have passed over, he has an honoured place.

There is no doubt that the tragedy they witnessed affected the Celtic players, and John Thomson's death had a deep and lasting impact on the football club.

Alec Thomson, like everyone else at the club, had to try and continue playing afterwards, but did so with heavy heart and mourning the loss of a friend and an outstanding goalkeeper.

AND ANOTHER THING ...

Wellesley Juniors proved to be a fruitful hunting ground for Celtic in the 1920s and 1930s, with a number of players coming to the club from there and proving their worth in the East End of Glasgow.

Alec Thomson was the first to arrive at the club, signing for Celtic in 1922 and spending twelve years at Celtic Park, making 451 appearances for the club and scoring 101 goals.

Celtic's next signing from the same club proved to be equally successful. John Thomson joined the club in 1926 after a year with Wellesley, and he had already made 188 appearances by the time of his tragic death in 1931. He was the greatest goalkeeper the club had seen up to that point and would have undoubtedly gone on to achieve truly great things in the game had his life not been cut short so cruelly.

His story remains the great tragedy of Celtic Football Club, while the tales of his prowess between the sticks has been passed down through the generations.

In 1930, Celtic recruited centre forward Frank O'Donnell from Wellesley. Over the next five years he would make 83 appearances for the club, scoring 58 goals, and for the last three years at Celtic Park he was joined by his younger brother, Hugh, another Wellesley graduate. He made 90 appearances for Celtic, scoring 27 goals.

Preston North End signed the two O'Donnell brothers in 1935, with Hugh following his brother out of Celtic Park when the Hoops would probably have preferred to keep him.

Joe Cowan was another Wellesley Juniors graduate, signed for Celtic after scoring twelve goals in five games for the Fife side, but he would only make one appearance for the Hoops.

That came in a league game against Aberdeen at Pittodrie in January 1931, when he scored in a 1–1 draw.

28

JOHN DIVERS

101 GOALS IN 232 APPEARANCES

It was perhaps destiny that John Divers would become a professional footballer and one who shone most brightly in the green and white Hoops of Celtic. His father, also John, had already played for the club between 1932 and 1945, making almost 200 appearances and scoring 92 goals.

Indeed, it would have been a remarkable achievement had father and son both made it into the list of Century Bhoys, even if half of Divers Senior's goals had come during wartime football.

As it was, John Divers the younger still found himself alongside family in this exclusive grouping because his great-uncle, Patsy Gallacher, was already there with an impressive 192 goals for the club between 1911 and 1926. Divers said:

> I was born and brought up in a house in Clydebank belonging to Madge Gallacher, my granny and my uncle Patsy's sister. I always remember there was plenty of talk in the house about Celtic and I remember my father and Patsy actually having quite heated conversations, because they were both strong-willed individuals, about football in general and Celtic in particular.

There had been already been a John Divers who had played for Celtic between 1893 and 1896, though he is no relation to the twentieth century father and son who wore the Hoops.

The nineteenth-century Bhoy played 87 times for the green and white stripes, scoring 40 goals for the club, and helping them win the league in 1894 and 1996.

He made one appearance for Scotland in a match against Wales in 1895, while John Divers' father also represented his country on one occasion, against Northern Ireland in 1939. There was to be no international recognition for the last of the trio.

Born in Clydebank in March 1940, the young John Divers attended school in nearby Dumbarton. He was spotted by Celtic, perhaps already eager to unearth 'the new Johnny Divers', and he joined the club in July 1956 before being farmed out to Renfrew Juniors.

Just over a year later, the teenager made his first-team debut for the Hoops and opened his scoring account with a goal in that game.

'Coming to Celtic Park in those days [1957] very few people even had televisions,' explained Divers, 'it was a different world.'

The star football players of that era, they weren't appearing on your TV screens every week, they were almost mystical figures and you would see their photographs in the papers or perhaps an action shot from one of the games, but you would never see them face-to-face, doing one-on-one interviews.

You really didn't know what to expect when you met the players for the first time, but they were just ordinary guys.

You never really got to know them well, because they were all around ten years older than me, but I just remember how nice they were. They were friendly, they were interested in you and you never came across anyone who fancied themselves. They would talk to you, encourage you, they were all nice people.

FIRST GOAL

It was a season of firsts for John Divers in 1957/58. He made his Celtic debut, he scored his first goal for the club and he made a solitary appearance for the first team that year. Of course, that means everything was rolled into one game and it was against St Mirren on 16 November 1957.

The seventeen-year-old inside-left found himself in the starting XI for the league match at Celtic Park and duly made his mark on the occasion when he scored after just twenty-one minutes to put Celtic 1–0 ahead.

It was an impressive start to his career with the Hoops, all the more so when you consider he was taking his place alongside the men who had beaten Rangers 7–1 in the League Cup final just a month before.

The teenager was in the team instead of Bobby Collins, but the rest of the line-up was the same as the famous one which had triumphed at Hampden, so to make his mark in that game and not be overawed, augured well for his future career.

That game against St Mirren finished 2–2, with Sammy Wilson scoring Celtic's other goal, and John Divers returned to the reserves, under the tutelage of Jock Stein, who was now coaching the team.

'I scored with a downward header at the non-Celtic End at Celtic Park and to be honest, I felt quite embarrassed,' said Divers of his first goal.

I didn't know what to do. Here was I playing with all these legendary Celtic figures, Willie Fernie, Bobby Evans, Bertie

Peacock, John McPhail and Neil Mochan and here was I at seventeen years of age, scoring a goal. I remember feeling embarrassed, but later on feeling quite proud of myself.

The following season, the player began to push him way into the first team on a more regular basis, making a total of 25 appearances and scoring 11 goals, one of four Celts to make it into double figures that season.

That tally included his first goal against Rangers, in a 2–1 Scottish Cup third-round victory when he headed Celtic into the lead just before half-time. Unfortunately, Celtic exited the tournament at the semi-final stage, going down 4–0 to St Mirren at Hampden.

The Hoops also finished a distant sixth in the league that season, a position indicative of Celtic's condition at that time, and while there were a number of promising young players emerging, including Divers, Mike Jackson, Bertie Auld, John Colrain, Billy McNeill and Pat Crerand, the club lacked direction and leadership and, as a result, tangible success in the form of silverware continued to elude them after reaching the heady heights of the 7–1 League Cup final triumph.

100TH GOAL

John Divers' 100th goal for Celtic is a significant one, not just for the player, but for the club as well. It represented the first goal of the 1965/66 league campaign when Celtic would go on to claim their first title in twelve years. More importantly, that championship was the first of nine-in-a-row, and Divers can thus rightly claim to have scored the very first goal of that historic sequence.

The goal came on the opening day of the season when Celtic,

now managed by Divers' former reserve coach, Jock Stein, travelled to Tannadice. The Hoops recorded an impressive 4–0 victory, with Divers opening the scoring after just fifteen minutes, and further goals from Joe McBride, Ian Young and Tommy Gemmell gave Stein's side the perfect start to the campaign.

It also provided a measure of revenge for the 2–1 defeat the Hoops had suffered against Dundee United in their first competitive match that season – the opening League Cup sectional match – and Celtic had already bounced back before meeting United again in the League.

A week before scoring his 100th goal for the club, Divers had provided a superb goal for Number 99 in a 1–0 League Cup victory over Motherwell at Celtic Park. His powerful shot on 68 minutes gave Stein's side the victory and would ultimately help them to progress beyond the sectional stage of the competition.

Divers was no longer a regular in the Celtic side, though he'd made seventeen appearances the previous season, including ten in the league. However, as the club entered a new era of unprecedented success, Divers' career in the Hoops was drawing to a close, though neither he nor anyone else for that matter would have realised just how successful the team was going to be under Stein.

LAST GOAL

Having managed to reach the magical 100-mark, John Divers would score one more goal for Celtic and it came on 4 September, 1965 at Dens Park, in a 3–1 League Cup win over Dundee.

The goal came after just eleven minutes and helped Stein's side gain both points, in the process ensuring they topped their section and qualified for the knockout stage of the competition.

Celtic would go all the way to the final that season, beating

Rangers 2–1 at Hampden courtesy of two John Hughes' penalties to lift the trophy, though Divers would play no further part in the campaign.

In fact, he made only two more appearances for the first team that season after scoring his final goal for the Hoops, and that came in consecutive league fixtures at home to Clyde and then away to Rangers.

That game at Ibrox finished in a 2–1 defeat, with John Hughes scoring from the spot. Celtic would gain a measure of revenge for that loss with a 5–1 victory on 3 January 1966, when Stevie Chalmers netted a hat-trick.

Divers remained at the club for the rest of the 1965/66 season and, as a Celtic supporter, as well as having been at the club throughout the barren years just past, he would have celebrated the success as much as anyone.

But by September 1966, he had moved to the north of the city, joining Partick Thistle, and although he played against Celtic on a handful of occasions over the next three seasons, John Divers didn't score against the Hoops.

HIGHS AND LOWS

For a player who made 232 appearances and scored 101 goals for Celtic, it's disappointing to reflect on the fact that John Divers won no major honours with the club. He made his debut a month after the famous 7–1 win and left a year before the even more famous 2–1 victory over Inter Milan in Lisbon.

There were a few trophies lifted during the latter stages of his career – the 1965 Scottish Cup and the League title the following season, along with the League Cup – but Divers didn't play in either final and only made three league appearances in the 1965/66 championship-winning campaign.

His time at the club was marked by a distinct lack of success, but it didn't prevent him from making an indelible mark on the club's history.

He also played alongside another Century Bhoy in the shape of Neilly Mochan, and always appreciated the help and advice the older man gave him throughout his time at the club.

'My father had actually moved to Morton after the war and I used to meet players like Couples and McGarrity, but one who stuck in my mind from that time was Neilly Mochan,' explained Divers.

My Dad always used to talk about Neilly, saying how happy and friendly he was, so when I came to Celtic Park at fifteen years of age and started training with these famous people, it might sound a bit naff to say it, but Neilly was a kind of father figure to me because he knew me. He was a confidant if you like.

Out of all his goals in the green and white Hoops, John Divers has a particular favourite. It came in a 4–3 victory over Hibernian on 16 December 1961 and was a momentous day for the player on and off the park.

'It's a fairly memorable day for me, because that was the day I got engaged and it happened to be the day we played Hibs at Celtic Park,' he explained.

In the last minute of the game, I scored from a cross from John Hughes with a diving header that beat Ronnie Simpson, who was the Hibs' goalkeeper. It was my third goal of the game and also the winning goal, so it stands as the most memorable goal of my career at Celtic.

AND ANOTHER THING ...

John Divers' football career took him from Celtic Park to Firhill, and he played for three years with Partick Thistle before retiring in 1969. By then a career in education beckoned, and after studying at Strathclyde University, he went on to become a teacher.

'Football became increasingly difficult for me, because ever since I was sixteen, I had been troubled by the circulation flow in my legs,' he explained.

I had been in hospital under a vascular surgeon, who said that I may have been twenty, but my legs were seventy.'

So when I was twenty-eight, my legs must have been eighty-five. So it was no great wrench for me to leave football and go into the world of education. I did play once or twice for the Strathclyde Faculty team, but that was just a bit of fun. But I really enjoyed the student life.

When I qualified I went on to teach in Braidhurst High in Motherwell, St Bride's in East Kilbride, but for almost thirty years I taught at Our Lady and St Pat's High in Dumbarton, formerly St Patrick's High and Notre Dame High.

I enjoyed what I would class as my biggest success in the football world at St Pat's High in 1988/89 when I took charge of the Under-15 football team. In the course of that season they played 28 games, of which we won 27 and drew one, although that was the quarter-final of the U15 Scottish Intermediate Shield and they won the replay in Edinburgh.

That team won the league, the Glasgow Cup and also the Scottish Cup and that gave me a great deal of pride. And may I say that I got out at the top. I've never taken a team since!

BIBLIOGRAPHY

Celtic View, various, (Celtic F.C., Glasgow, 1965–).

Potter, David, *Tommy McInally, Celtic's Bad Bhoy?*, (Black & White Publishing Ltd, Edinburgh, 2009).